GARAGES

Complete Step-by-Step
Building Plans

Affectionately dedicated to
Ray and Michele

GARAGES

Complete Step-by-Step Building Plans

Ernie Bryant

TAB BOOKS
Blue Ridge Summit, PA

FIRST EDITION
THIRD PRINTING

© 1990 by **TAB BOOKS**.
TAB BOOKS is a division of McGraw-Hill, Inc.

Library of Congress Cataloging-in-Publication Data

Bryant, Ernie.
    Garages : complete step-by-step building plans / Ernie Bryant.
      p.   cm.
   ISBN 0-8306-9214-2   ISBN 0-8306-3314-6 (pbk.)
    1. Garages—Design and construction—Amateurs' manuals.
   2. Garages—Designs and plans. I. Title.
   TH4960.B78   1989
   690'.89—dc20   89-36598
                                     CIP

TAB BOOKS offers software for sale. For information and a catalog, please contact TAB Software Department, Blue Ridge Summit, PA 17294-0850.

Questions regarding the content of this book should be addressed to:

Reader Inquiry Branch
TAB BOOKS
Blue Ridge Summit, PA 17294-0850

Acquisitions Editor: Kimberly Tabor
Book Editor: Lori Flaherty
Paperbound Cover Design: Lori E. Schlosser

Contents

Acknowledgments

I would like to thank the following people: Rick Lamarre, a fine artist with a knowledge of building construction. He offered many ideas regarding the layout of the illustrations.

Donald and Jean Marcy, who were kind enough to let me take pictures of their garage in various stages of construction. Because of photography problems, however, I was unable to use the pictures in this book.

William Salwocki, General Manager of Home Designing Service in New Britain, Connecticut, who provided the foreword for this book.

Foreword

Over the past two decades, the types of home improvement projects the typical home handyman tackled have changed. Twenty years ago, a weekend project was usually limited to cleaning the gutters or painting the house. It used to be that when there was a plumbing problem, a plumber was called, an electrical problem required an electrician, and a carpenter was hired for your building projects.

Not so anymore. Today, homeowners realize the value in learning how to fix and build things themselves. Whether the need is for a new ceiling fan, replacing a kitchen sink, or building a new patio or deck, the weekend project has evolved into a more complex, sometimes multi-weekend undertaking.

The emergence of the super large hardware/lumber yard retail stores is further evidence of the extent homeowners are doing more handyman work. Small local hardware stores and lumberyards that once catered to the professional tradesman and contractor now face stiff competition from the new "home center," the super large hardware/lumber yard retail stores with supplies, ideas, projects, and how-to books for the do-it-yourselfer. These new "home centers" are catering to homeowners and encouraging them to learn how to do more home improvement projects themselves.

In his new book, *Garages: Complete Step-by-Step Building Plans*, Ernie Bryant has provided the instructions for the ambitious do-it-yourselfer to tackle the project of building a garage. Building a complete garage is, without a doubt, a large undertaking, but with the proper information and instructions, the average handyman can do it. Ernie's book provides this information and the necessary how-to instructions.

This book takes you through all the stages of building a garage—excavation, foundation work, carpentry layout, and other aspects of successfully building a garage are covered. Each plan includes complete dimensions, details, materials list, and framing plans to make construction go as smoothly as possible.

This book can also be very helpful to the seasoned carpenter contractor. It has five garage plans and more than 120 illustrations, with many ideas and styles that can be used to show clients the various sizes and styles of garages that can be built.

Ernie Bryant has worked for Home Designing Service for several years as a custom home designer. He is well qualified and experienced in residential design. His experience has helped many of our clients, and I know that his new book will help many people successfully build a garage.

William J. Salwocki
General Manager
Home Designing Service

Introduction

If you've ever thought about building a garage, then this book is for you. If you've ever thought about building a garage with living quarters above it, then this book is for you. And if you've ever thought about remodeling the upper portion of your existing garage, then this book is also for you.

The purpose of this book is to explain the step-by-step procedures in constructing a garage. One chapter explains how to locate corners and build batter boards. Another chapter discusses concrete pouring. Also discussed are framing, roof installation, installing gypsum board, installing paneling, flooring, electrical, and plumbing.

This is truly a garage building book. My previous book, The Building Plan Book, with complete working drawings for 21 houses, was well received. It was then that I realized there was a need for a garage building book.

In addition to text, details, and illustrations, this book includes complete working drawings for various garages. For instance, there are plans for a three-car garage and there are plans for a three-car garage with living quarters above it. There are also plans for a two-car garage, a two-car garage with living quarters above it, and a one-car garage.

You could go to an architect and have him/her draw up a set of plans for you, or you could go to a designing service. A designing service will have stock plans of garages or they could custom design a garage for you. Working drawings can also be obtained from a competent draftsman who works independently, or you could order plans through the mail.

But if one of the plans in this book interests you, you can save a great deal of money. You will need about six to ten sets of plans by the time you're done with construction. The bank gets one, the building inspector gets one, the concrete contractor gets one, the framers get one, the electrician gets one, and you're going to lose one or one is going to get damaged.

If you are going to build one of the structures in this book, just go to your nearest duplicating machine and make as many copies of the plans as you will need.

Each set of garage building plans include the following:

1. Perspective—A three-quarter view of the garage.
2. Floor Plans—Exterior door and window dimensions, interior wall dimensions, direction of floor joist or ceiling joists, and rafters.
3. Foundation Plan—Shows the thickness of the foundation wall and footing, and the location of lally columns.
4. Section—A cut-away view of the structure detailing how it is constructed.
5. Front Elevation—Front view of the garage.
6. Right Elevation—Right view of the garage.
7. Rear Elevation—Rear view of the structure.
8. Left Elevation—Left view of the structure.
9. Framing Plans—Details lumber sizes and their location.
10. Electrical Layout—Shown on floor plans. It shows the location of switches, outlets, and lights.
11. Materials List—List of building materials needed to construct the garage.

The materials list, which is included with each building plan, tells you how many studs, joists, rafters, etc. are needed to construct the garage. For example, if the material list states 2×10------16/12, it means that 16, two-by-ten wood members, 12 feet long, are needed.

Throughout the text, reference is made to various nail sizes by the symbol 8d, 6d, etc. The 8d is read as eight penny, 6d is read as six penny, etc.

A WORD ABOUT SAFETY

All of the plans in this book have been designed with safety in mind. The size of beams, joists, and rafters are based on their span and the load they must support. If the plans call for two-by-ten floor joists, sixteen inches on center, there is a good reason for it. Do not try to save a few dollars by substituting smaller wood members that might be inadequate. If you intend to use the plans in this book but would like to enlarge the structure, have a competent architectural draftsperson or architect look over the plans. If you enlarge a garage in such a way that the joists, rafters, or beam is lengthened, you must also increase the size of those wood members accordingly. An architect or architectural draftsperson will be able to calculate the proper size of the lengthened wood member.

Regarding safety, I've done what I can in designing the garage plans. It is up to you to excercise proper safety procedures during the construction phase. Although this book was written for the homeowner and the do-it-yourselfer, if there is something you don't understand or have doubts about whether or not you can do it, hire a professional. Pouring a concrete slab is quite an undertaking. If you can get a few guys who are willing to spend the day doing hard work pouring the slab, that is great. But if you can't get anyone to help you, it would be wise to hire a professional. When you are working on the roof, tie a rope around your waist. Of course, that won't do any good unless the other end is tied around something that will prevent you from reaching the ground in the event you should fall.

Wear protective clothing and safety goggles when working with insulation or other hazardous materials and tools. Always use common sense. Take safety precautions. Exercise proper safety procedures.

1

Tools

___

Tool selectivity is the key to good carpentry. There are many different types of tools available. The variety of high-quality tools available for doing common building projects helps make your work easier because you can select the proper tool for the job. Tool quality is also important. High-quality tools last longer than cheaply-made tools. Good tools are usually made from better materials and are lighter and stronger than bargain tools. It is important to keep good tools clean, properly lubricated, and in good working condition.

CLAW HAMMERS

If you are reading this book, most likely you know what a claw hammer is, but did you know that there are two main types? The two types I refer to in this book are the curved claw and the ripping claw. The ripping claw is fairly straight and is used mainly to pull or rip pieces apart. The rounded claw of the curved claw hammer offers more leverage for pulling nails.

The hammer faces are made flat or slightly convex. The convex type enbles you to drive a nail flush without damaging the surface of the wood. The mesh type is used for framing work. The length of the handle is determined by the kind of work you plan to do. Long handles provide more leverage than shorter ones and are used for framing work. The weight of the head can vary from five to 20 ounces. Generally, a 14 or 16-ounce head is used for finishing, while a 16 to 20-ounce head is preferred for framing work.

STAPLES

As an alternative to using a hammer, a power-driven stapler can make some carpentry jobs easier. These lightweight staples can be slammed or squeezed against the surface which is to be fastened. They are handy for fastening insulation, ceiling tiles, or housewrap in place.

SCREWDRIVERS

In addition to the hammer, the screwdriver is one of the most frequently used tool of a homeowner. Although it is a common tool, there are some situations where an ordinary screwdriver will not work. There are times when you will need a Phillips screwdriver for a Phillips screw. Your tool box should contain three or four screwdrivers of varying sizes. If a screwdriver is too small or too big it could burr the screw head or damage the work. Don't use a faulty screwdriver that is so worn and blunted that the tempered tip is damaged.

When purchasing a screwdriver, select one with a square shank. In the event that you have difficulty with a stubborn screw, you can apply extra leverage by fitting a wrench on the square shank. More power can be applied with a long screwdriver than a short one, which has a tip the same size. Smaller screwdrivers are ideal if you have limited work space.

SAWS

Like other tools, saws are designed according to how they will be used.

Handsaw

The type of cutting a handsaw can do is determined by the shape of the saw, the blade size, and the number and position of teeth along the blade. A 12-point saw has 12 teeth per inch. The term point refers to the number of teeth per inch. The smaller the teeth, the finer the cut. The teeth on a saw are bent outward to obtain a cut that is wider than the blade. This enables the blade to move forward and backward smoothly.

Crosscut Saw

A saw that is widely used is the crosscut saw. It is capable of cutting across wood grain and is used for cutting plywood and other wood-base materials. Its teeth have a cutting edge on both sides. When using a crosscut saw, it should be used at a 45 degree angle to the surface. The teeth cut on the forward stroke.

Ripsaw

The chisel type of teeth of the ripsaw enable it to cut quickly in line with wood grain. It has four to six teeth per inch on the blade. It is best to hold the ripsaw at a 60 degree angle when cutting.

Backsaw

If you're going to do finish work where it is important to cut straight lines, use a backsaw. It has 11 to 16 teeth per blade-inch and is held parallel to the cutting surface.

Compass Saw

Used for making curves and cut-outs, the compass saw has a 12-inch blade that is pointed at the end, and less than an inch at the base. It should be held perpendicular to the surface when cutting curves.

Coping Saw

With its thin blade held taut in a small rectangular frame, the coping saw makes accurate cuts and can saw tight curves with ease. The cutting is done on the pull stroke, because the teeth point toward the handle.

PLANES

The purpose of a plane is to eliminate unwanted portions of wood. Unlike a chisel, the body of the plane controls the depth and width of the cut. The two most commonly used planes are the bench plane and the block plane. A block plane is small enough to hold in one hand and is used for planing rounded surfaces and for planing end grain. The bench plane is used along the board's length for smoothing with the grain.

FOLDING WOODEN RULE

Constructed of six or eight-inch wooden sections, which are hinged together, the folding rule is a very accurate tool. It can be extended to obtain a measurement without someone holding the other end. A sliding extension makes it possible to obtain precise measurements.

SQUARES

A square is no good if it is not accurate. To keep it from rusting, occasionally wipe the blade with an oily rag.

Try Square

The blade of a try square, which is available in lengths of three to 15 inches, is helpful when laying out right angles and testing to make sure your work is square. To determine the squareness of a board edge, place the handle of the try square along one surface. Slide the blade into contact with the board edge. If light can be seen between the blade and the board, the edge is untrue. Sand or plane until the board edge is square and true.

Combination Square

Many jobs can be done with a combination square. It can be used as a try square, level, miter gauge, plumb, or gauging tool. The free-sliding 12-inch rule can be tightened to the blade or removed. A spirit level, for checking true level and plumb, is built into the combination square.

Framing Square

The sides of both blades of a framing square are inscribed with useful tables and scales and can be used as a reference when laying out rafters, computing board feet, and measuring in 10ths or 100ths of an inch. The most commonly-used framing square has a 12-inch tongue and an 18-inch body and is available in polished nickel, copper, and blued finishes.

LEVEL

Just as its name implies, the level is used to check the true level of horizontal surfaces. It can also be used for checking vertical surfaces for plumb. Levels are made of wood, aluminum, or lightweight alloys. In the center of the tool is a glass tube which holds an air bubble in water. The surface is level when the lines on the tube's surface exactly frame the bubble. At each end of the tool, a similar tube indicates plumb.

PLUMB BOB

True plumb can also be checked by the use of a plumb bob. This consists of a heavy, pointed weight which is suspended from a length of string. With the end of the string held high, and the bob a fraction of an inch above the ground, true plumb can be determined.

NAILS

Common nails and box nails are similar except box nails are thinner. The thinner box nail is less likely to split the wood, although it bends more easily when not hammered properly.

A casing nail or finish nail should be used for finish work. A casing nail is a little heavier and stronger; a countersunk finish nail leaves a smaller hole to fill.

A scaffold nail is ideal to use on a temporary structure that will later be taken apart.

All of these nails can be found in most stores in sizes ranging from 2d (two penny) to 16d (sixteen penny). Many years ago, the term penny referred to the cost of a hundred hand-forged nails. Today, the term penny indicates a nail's length and is denoted with the small letter d.

Rustproof Nails

When you are nailing siding to the exterior of a garage, it is a good idea to use nonferrous or stainless steel nails. Galvanized nails will eventually rust. Aluminum nails are ideal for exterior work and are inexpensive. Stainless steel nails can be expensive, but are more commonly used on exterior siding.

Masonry Nails

Available in various sizes, masonry nails can be driven into concrete, concrete block, brick, soft stone, and other masonry. When these high-carbon nails are driven into seasoned concrete, they maintain lateral holding power but have little holding power on any outward pull.

2

Foundation

WHEN DETERMINING THE SIZE OF A GARAGE, AN IMPORTANT consideration is comfortable access to both sides of the vehicle. The minimum size of a one-car garage is 10 feet × 20 feet, however, this only permits access to one side of the car. Increasing the size of the garage by 2 feet in both directions allows easy access to both sides of the vehicle. A recommended size for a two-car garage is 22 feet × 22 feet. If you plan to have a work area or storage space, the size should be adjusted accordingly.

Garage doors are usually overhead doors that roll upward. Whether the sectional roll-up type or the one-piece swing-up type is used, the amount of room needed for the door track assembly should be considered when determining the ceiling height of the garage. Although there are a number of stock sizes, the most common garage door is nine feet by seven feet. A large, single garage door, 16 feet by seven feet, can be substituted, but two individual doors allow more accurate placement of the cars.

The garage floor is usually a four-inch thick concrete slab, which should be pitched toward a floor drain or toward the door at $1/8$ inch per foot. The top of the slab should also be four inches below the top of the foundation to prevent snow and rain from entering.

A single door to enable people to enter without having to open large garage doors is desirable. Windows are also desirable for providing natural light.

If your garage will have living quarters above, firecode

gypsum board must be applied on ceilings and walls. Check with your local building codes.

THE STRING/ARC METHOD

To locate the corners of the building to be constructed, determine the location of one corner, which for the purpose of illustration is referred to as Corner One. From this corner, measure 30 feet in a straight line. Then drive a stake into the ground, which will be referred to as Point R. See Fig. 2-1.

Using string with a piece of chalk tied to one end of it, place one end of the string on the stake at Point R. Then draw an arc on the ground in a 50 foot radius. After this is done,

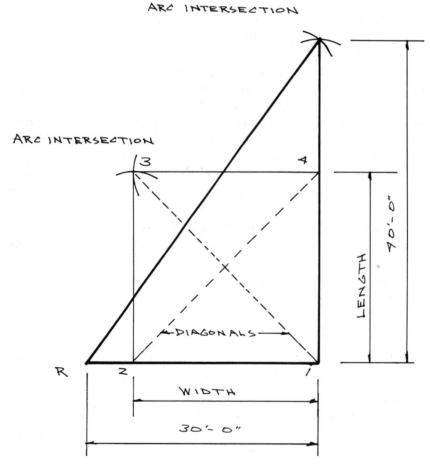

Fig. 2-1. *Locating corners with the string/arc method.*

place the end of the string on the stake at Corner One, and using the chalk and string, draw an arc in a 40 foot radius. Place a stake at the intersection of the two arcs. Point R, Corner One, and the arcs intersection form a triangle that assumes square corners.

Stretch a line from the stake at the intersection of the arcs to the first corner. Then run the string from Corner One to Point R. The nails in the center of the stake will hold the lines taut.

Starting at Corner One and going toward Point R, measure the width of the garage and drive a stake, establishing Corner Two. Now measure from Corner One toward the arcs intersection, the length of the garage, and drive a stake. This establishes Corner Four.

Using a string that is equal to the length of the sides of the garage, draw an arc from Corner Two. Using a line that is equal to the width of the front of the garage, draw an arc from Corner Four. The intersection of the two arcs determine the location of Corner Three. Drive a stake at this corner.

To determine if the layout lines are square, stretch diagonals across the stakes. The building layout lines are square if the diagonal lines are equal.

BATTER BOARDS

Batter boards are used to record horizontal reference points (away from the construction), such as footing and foundation walls. Structures built with precision should have batter boards to record the points of buildings, walls, etc.

After deciding what grade level to maintain around the garage, drive a stake flush into the ground at that level. Drive a nail into the top of the stake so that it projects about one inch above the stake. This stake is to be referred to as the grade level stake. Tie a line to the nail, place a line level on it, and stretch it to various points within the area of construction. This will indicate where to remove soil and where to fill it in.

Drive a finishing nail into the top of the stake that represents Corner One. Approximately 3 feet from the corner stake, drive three stakes into the ground as batter board stakes. Stretch a line from the grade level stake to the batter board stakes. Position the line level on the line, then, using a pencil,

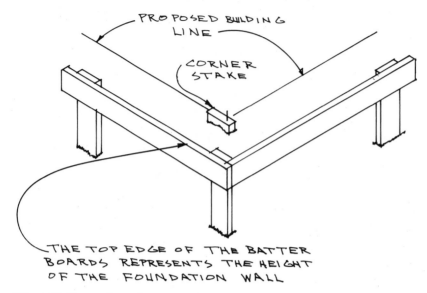

Fig. 2-2. Batter boards.

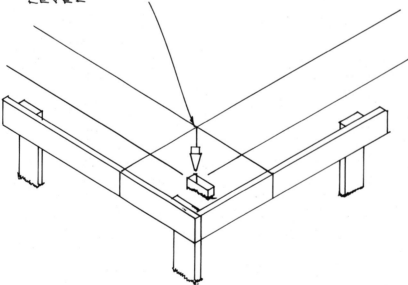

Fig. 2-3. Batter board strings and plumb lines.

mark the stakes where the line is level. Nail the batter boards to the batter board stakes at the proper height. The top edge of the batter board represents the top edge of the foundation wall, see Fig. 2-2. Erect batter boards the same way at the other corners of the structure to be built.

With a plumb bob, stretch a line directly over the finishing nail in the corner stake. Hold the point of the plumb bob over the nail in the corner stake. The foundation line should touch the plumb bob line. To maintain a taut line, wrap it around the batter boards. This line indicates the top outside edge of the foundation wall, see Fig. 2-3.

Footing and Foundation

Check your local building codes to determine the depth that the foundation footing has to be below grade. Measure the

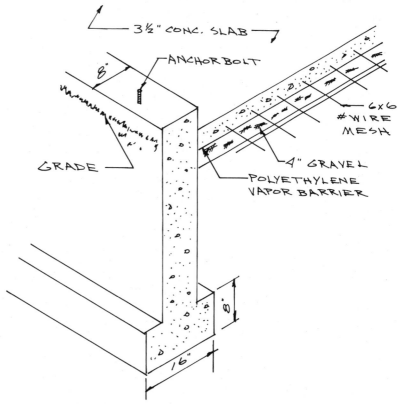

Fig. 2-4. *Cut-away view of the foundation wall.*

required depth from the guide line, see Fig. 2-4. Make sure the bottom of the trench is level by using the straight edge of a two by four wood member and a carpenter level. A foundation wall constructed of concrete block is not recommended in northern climates where frost heave is a problem. Constructing a concrete block foundation wall is discussed later in this chapter.

FORM BUILDING

Put alignment strings on all batter boards in place. These strings represent the outside face of the footing and the inside face of the forms. Where the string lines intersect, hang a plumb bob to the bottom of the excavation, see Fig. 2-5. At this spot, drive a stake then raise the plumb bob so it hangs over the stake without coming into contact with it.

Mark the exact point on the stake with a pencil. This point accurately represents the location of the outside corner of the footing. Nail a 6d nail into the mark on the stake; let enough of

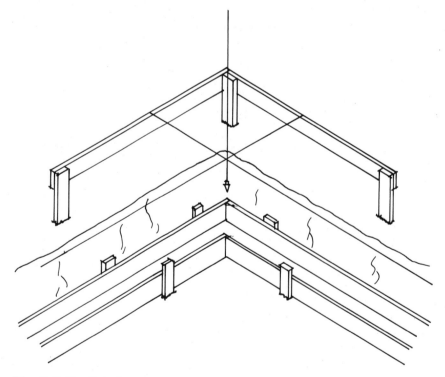

Fig. 2-5. *Footing forms.*

the nail protrude so a string can be attached. Repeat this process on all four corners. Stretch a string from each nail to outline the outside edge of the footing, and the inside face of the forms.

You can use 2 × 4 wood members, sharpened at one end, as form stakes. They should be 1 foot longer than the depth of the footing, so that the stake can be hammered one foot into the ground.

Beginning several inches from a corner, drive form stakes into the ground while proceeding around the string outline. The type of form material used will determine the spacing of the form stakes. Remove the string after the form stakes are in place.

Make a mark on any driven stake to denote the top of the footing. Stretch a line from the mark on the stake to the next stake. After leveling it with a line level, make a mark on the next stake. By repeating this process around the perimeter, the top of the footing form is established.

After putting the form boards in place, frequently check to make sure they are level. Then put the stakes so they are level with the top of the forms.

CONCRETE TYPES

Concrete gets its strength from the structural mixture of aggregate, bonded together by cement paste, which holds the crushed stone, gravel, and sand together. It is crucial to use the right amount of these elements and the proper amount of water. The water should be drinkable to ensure against organic matter. If too much water is used, the cement paste will be too thin to bond the aggregate together. If too little water is used, tiny pockets of dry aggregate will weaken the concrete.

A commonly-used cement is portland cement, of which there are various types.

Type I generates considerable heat during the curing process. This makes it ideal for cold weather because the heat helps to prevent it from freezing.

Type II gives off less heat in curing and is used in high temperatures.

Type III is useful in cold temperatures because it reduces

the cost of keeping the concrete protected against the cold during curing.

For cold areas it is recommended that air-entrained cement be used. Air-entrained cement consists of an agent that enables the finished concrete to be filled with many tiny air bubbles. The bubbles enable the water to freeze and expand without causing damage to the concrete. This type of cement can be used in regions that have severe frost.

POURING CONCRETE

The footing, which supports the foundation wall, should be just as thick and twice as wide. For example, an eight-inch foundation wall should have a footing that is eight inches deep and 16 inches wide. See Fig. 2-6.

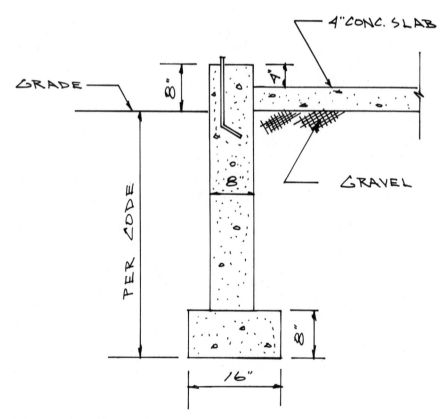

Fig. 2-6. *Foundation detail.*

The concrete for the footing should be a mixture of one part cement, three parts sand, and five parts gravel. Flush concrete around stones that have been placed in the footing form. Concrete should be kept wet to eliminate pockets. Work concrete into all corners, then level footing, using a two by four wood member as a screed across the forms.

Use a special concrete hoe or a square-ended shovel to place concrete in the footing forms and the foundation wall forms. A concrete rake can also be used for tamping.

All concrete should rest on undisturbed soil. The soil should have a minimum bearing capacity of 4,000 pounds per square foot.

Curing is an important factor in structural concrete. The purpose of it is to influence the rate of the chemical reaction between the water and the cement. The concrete should have a minimum compressive strength of 2,500 pounds per square inch at 28 days.

POURING GARAGE FLOOR

The garage concrete floor can be poured before framing or after. See Illustration 2-1. The floor should be four inches thick to accomodate cars. The top of the concrete slab should be four inches below the top of the foundation wall.

After leveling the gravel, place polyethylene vapor barrier over the entire floor area. Then roll out 6×6 reinforcing wire.

Keep in mind that the garage floor should pitch 1/8 inch per foot toward a drain or the garage door for drainage. If the garage floor is 24 feet in depth, the form at the back should be three inches higher than the front. Place a length of 1 1/2-inch $\times$ 1 1/2-inch angle iron across the garage door opening. About every two feet, drill and countersink holes in the angle iron to allow positioning of two-inch flathead screws in the concrete.

After the concrete is poured, screed the surface with a two by four wood member. Before the concrete sets, a bull float should be used to float the surface. The float removes excess water from the surface of the concrete and eliminates the ridges left from the screeding process.

Illustrated by Rick Lamarre

Illustration 2-1. *Pouring concrete.*

CONCRETE BLOCK FOUNDATION

Because mortar is important in masonry construction, make sure that you have the proper mix for the job. Do not mix more mortar than you can use in one hour. If the mortar becomes dried out, do not use it. Mortar generally consists of cement, hydrated lime, sand, and water.

Establish Spacing

To establish spacing, lay the first course of concrete blocks without mortar on the concrete footing. The joints can be increased or decreased to allow for slight inconsistencies in block lengths.

First Course

In a full bed of mortar, lay the first block where you want it on the concrete footing. The ends of the second block should be buttered with mortar and set next to the first block, thereby assuring good joints. Make sure the blocks are level, then butter and lay a few more blocks equal to the length of your level. After making sure the blocks are all level, repeat the process for the first course.

Corner Leads

The perimeter of the garage will be outlined after the first course has been laid. The second course is started at the corner. Place a block overlapping the two, butting blocks at the corner of the first course. One end of the block will be aligned with the outside edge of the face wall, and the other end will extend halfway over the adjacent block in the first course. This is the beginning of the staggered, running bond pattern. Several courses of corner leads should be built-up above the base course. Each block should be checked for level and plumb, and alignment at the outside surfaces.

Alignment

A string, which is strung corner to corner, is used as a guide to align the top, outside edge of the blocks. Move the string up for each course. The top of the blocks should be aligned with the string and leveled by tapping with the trowel handle to get the block edges in line. Then check with the level, again. See Fig. 2-7.

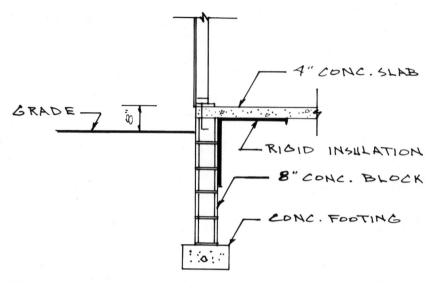

Fig. 2-7. *Concrete block foundation.*

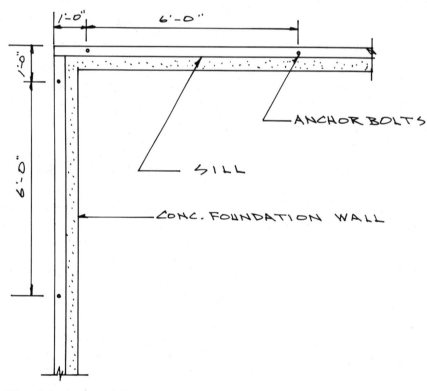

Fig. 2-8. *Anchor bolt placement.*

SILL PLACEMENT

A 2 × 6-inch sill should be anchored to the top of the foundation wall with anchor bolts. Position two by six wood members along the foundation. Locate and drill holes to receive anchor bolts. Oversize holes allow leeway in fastening the sill in the exact position. The sill must be kept flush with the outside edge of the foundation. See Fig. 2-8. Countersink anchor bolts into the sill, to allow easy positioning of the frame wall. Place the sill seal between the sill and the top of the foundation wall.

Figure 2-9 depicts a basic 3-4-5 triangle, which can be built in a number of multiple dimensions. It is used to measure the squareness of corners.

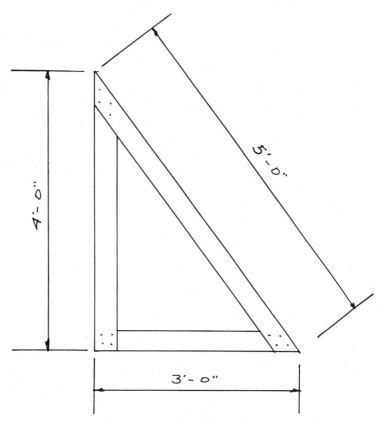

Fig. 2-9. *A basic 3-4-5 triangle can be built to measure the squareness of the corners.*

TRANSIT-LEVEL METHOD

Instead of using the string-arc method, you might prefer to use a transit-level to lay out the corners of your garage. The purpose of a transit-level is to measure horizontal angles accurately, as well as measuring the differences in elevation. Straight reference lines can also be obtained with a transit. This information is very helpful when laying out foundation footings that are square at the corners and level.

The transit-level is basically a telescope that can measure horizontal and vertical angles accurately. It has a spirit-level that can be leveled with four adjustable screws. The legs of the tripod are adjustable, and assure steady footing on most surfaces. A plumb-line hook is mounted directly under the tripod head. With the use of a plumb-line and a plumb bob, the transit can be centered over reference points such as a corner stake. See Fig. 2-10.

To use the transit-level, set it over the first corner stake with the legs approximately three feet apart. Adjust the legs so that the base plate of the transit, which attaches to the tripod,

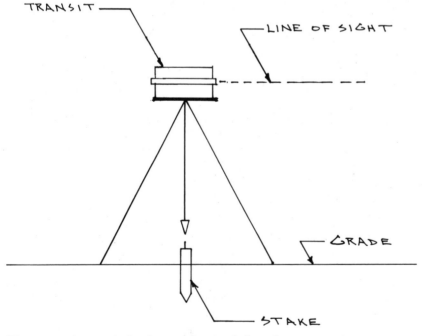

Fig. 2-10. *A transit-level provides straight reference.*

looks level. The center of the base plate is to be centered over the nail in the stake. With the plumb-line attached to the tripod hook, suspend the plumb bob over the nail in the stake without letting it come in contact with the nail.

After the transit is centered over the reference point it must be leveled. Use four leveling screws to level the bubble in the spirit-level, mounted 90 degrees apart. By turning two screws at a time, in opposite directions, the bubble in the spirit-level can be moved one way or the other. After turning the telescope 90 degrees, level the bubble again with the opposite pair of leveling screws. If this procedure causes the plumb-line and plumb bob to move off center, the plumb bob must be re-centered over the nail and the instrument leveled again.

Using a site plan, locate the location of the building corners with stakes. Level and center the transit over the first corner of the garage. The telescope should be focused along the line of one side of the garage. A leveling rod is a large, graduated scale that is held by an assistant just beyond the corner of the garage. As you look through the telescope, instruct your assistant to maneuver the leveling rod so it is in line with the line of sight of the telescope. Once the rod is in its proper place, have your assistant suspend a plumb bob on a line as it hangs above the rod. This will locate the line of sight for the side of the building. Mark the point on the ground and stake it. Because this stake is beyond the actual corner of the structure, it will be necessary to measure the distance from the reference point toward the stake. After moving the stake to the exact corner, use a metal tape to spot and pencil mark the top of the stake. This mark should be denoted with a 4d or 6d nail.

After the first corner of the garage is accurately located, turn the transit-level 90 degrees and focus along the front line of the garage. Repeat the layout procedure for the front of the garage. To locate the final corner of the garage, move the transit to the second corner of the front of the building and sight along the second side of the garage. Relevel and recenter the transit-level each time it is moved. Check for squareness at the corners by stretching a line across the diagonals of the garage corners. If the garage is square, the diagonals will be equal. The basic 3-4-5 triangle can also be used to measure the squareness of the corners.

3

Framing

A 2 × 4 WOOD MEMBER ACTUALLY MEASURES $1\frac{1}{2}$ × $3\frac{1}{2}$ IN-ches, a half-inch less in both directions. This is because of the method lumber is prepared for the market.

Years ago, air-drying was the accepted way of reducing the moisture content of lumber. Today, lumber is kiln-dried, a faster method than air-drying. The kiln-drying method, how-ever, increases the amount of shrinkage. Although the thick-ness and the width are affected by the increase in shrinkage, the length remains unchanged.

Milling is the process of dressing the lumber after it is cut to its rough size. Lumber is milled on all four surfaces, which results in a smooth piece of wood. This milling process also ac-counts for part of the shrinkage.

FRAMING THE WALLS

When building frame walls, always use the straightest wood members for the studs, shoe, and plate. Make sure that each piece of lumber is square.

When constructing a frame wall, place the plate and shoe together on a flat surface. Square the ends, then measure every 16 inches. Draw a line across the plate and shoe with a carpen-ters' square. The line represents the placement of each stud.

Using 16d nails, nail the shoe and one plate to each stud. See Fig. 3-1. A frame wall is considered square when the diago-nal measurements are equal in length. To keep the frame wall square, temporarily nail a one inch by six inch wood member

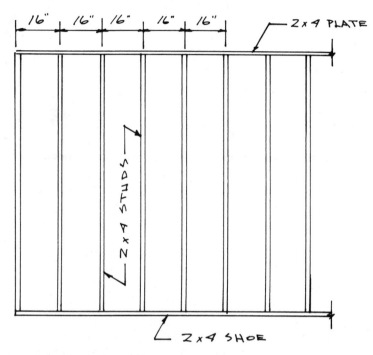

Fig. 3-1. *Stud framing wall.*

across the studs. After the frame is constructed, you will need help to raise and brace it into position. See Illustration 3-1.

To make sure that the frames are level and plumb, place a rule over the end of the plate. Allow it to project two inches, then drop a plumb line over the end of it. When the distance from the plumb line to the shoe is the same as the distance from the plumb line to the plate, the frame is plumb in that direction. See Fig. 3-2. Check both directions. Use one-inch by six-inch braces to keep the frames plumb. The braces can be nailed from a stud to a stake in the ground.

DOOR AND WINDOW ROUGH OPENINGS

The rough opening height for door and windows is six feet and nine inches from the floor. This measurement dictates the placement of the bottom of the door or window header. See Fig. 3-3. The size of the header is determined by the span of the rough opening and the weight it must support. The window and door headers are supported by jack studs. The rough opening of windows and doors are spec-

24

Illustration 3-1. *Erecting the stud wall.*

Illustrated by Rick Lamarre

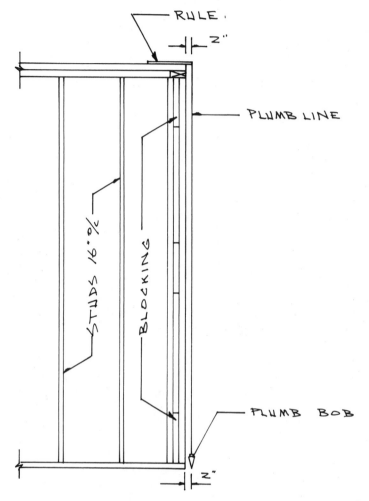

Fig. 3-2. Frame walls must be level and plumb.

ified by the manufacturer. Frame openings to the proper size. See Fig.
3-4.

SECOND FLOOR FRAMING

If the garage is to have a second floor, (see Fig. 3-5), it will
need to have a beam and vertical supports. The beam is usually
positioned in the center of the garage. The size of the beam is
determined by the unsupported span and the load it must support. The lally columns, which support the beam, are placed on

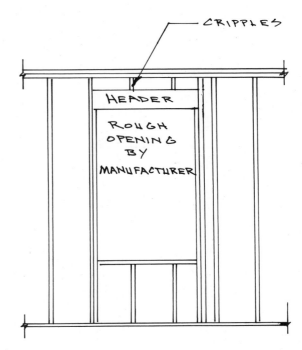

Fig. 3-3. *Window rough opening.*

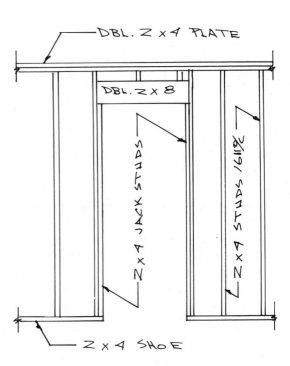

Fig. 3-4. *Door rough opening.*

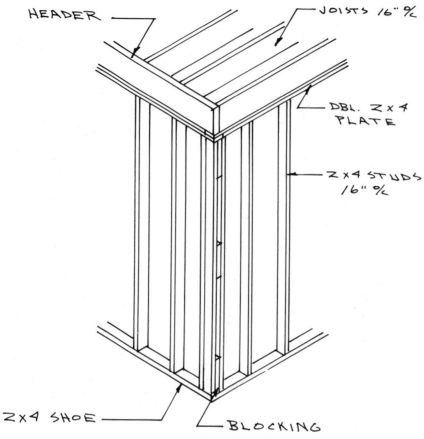

HEADER

JOISTS 16" %

DBL. 2 x 4 PLATE

2 x 4 STUDS 16" %

2 x 4 SHOE

BLOCKING

Fig. 3-5. *Corner detail.*

concrete footings beneath the garage floor slab. See Fig. 3-6. The further apart the lally columns are, the bigger the beam will be.

The size of the floor joists are also determined by the unsupported span and the weight it must carry. See Fig. 3-7.

The header, or box header, should be toenailed in position on both sides. Then drive 16d nails through the header into the floor joists, which should be positioned every 16 inches. See Fig. 3-8.

One row of 1 × 3-inch bridging should be positioned between the floor joists per span. See Fig. 3-9.

Use double joists under parallel partitions. Use double studs when perpendicular partitions meet. See Fig. 3-10.

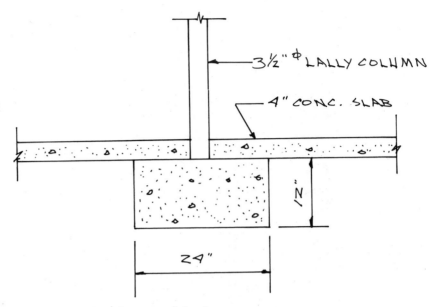

Fig. 3-6. *Lally column and footing.*

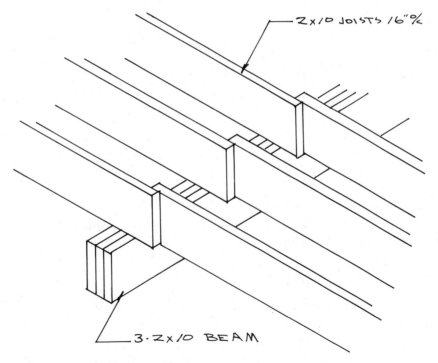

Fig. 3-7. *Joists and beams.*

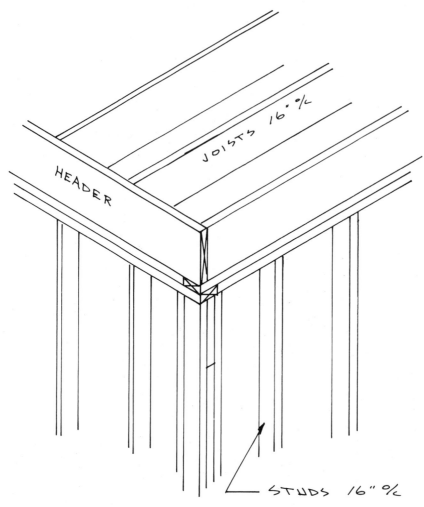

Fig. 3-8. *Plate and header corner detail.*

Finally, assemble corners to allow nailing power for the gypsum board. See Fig. 3-11.

WALL SHEATHING

Plywood sheathing should be applied horizontally or vertically to the framing (to strengthen the structure and provide insulation). See Illustration 3-2. When installing wall sheathing leave 1/8-inch space at the panel joints and a 1/16-inch space

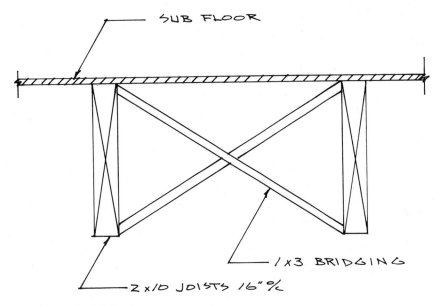

SUB FLOOR

1 x 3 BRIDGING

2 x 10 JOISTS 16" ℀

Fig. 3-9. *Bridging.*

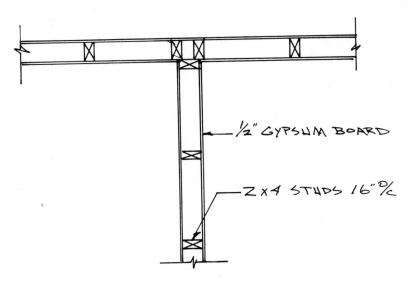

½" GYPSUM BOARD

2 x 4 STUDS 16" ℀

Fig. 3-10. *Double studs at perpendicular partitions.*

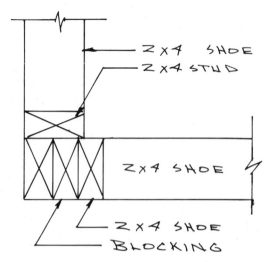

2 X 4 SHOE
2 X 4 STUD

2 X 4 SHOE

2 X 4 SHOE
BLOCKING

Fig. 3-11. *Plan view of corner.*

Illustration 3-2. *Applying sheathing.*

between panel end joints. Along the edge, place 8d nails 6 to 10 inches apart and 12 to 16 inches on inner studs.

ASPHALT FELT

Apply 15# Asphalt Felt or air infiltration housewrap to the wall sheathing. See Fig. 3-12. Each course of felt should overlap two inches.

HOUSEWRAP

Housewrap, a sheet of high-density polyethylene fibers, is available in nine-foot wide rolls and three-foot wide rolls. Housewrap is rolled across the entire structure. Starting at one corner of the structure, wrap a roll of housewrap around corners, doors, and window openings. See Illustration 3-3. The

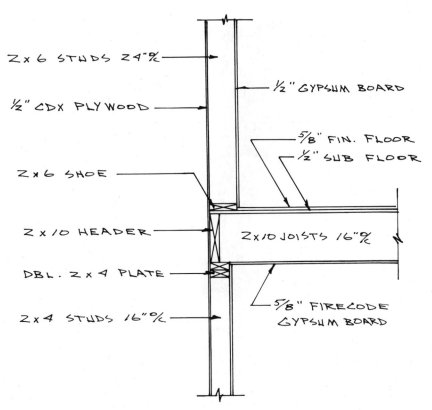

Fig. 3-12. *Second floor framing detail.*

Illustration 3-3. *Applying housewrap.*

Illustrated by Rick Lamarre

housewrap is then pulled over the frames of the rough openings of doors and windows.

CEILING JOISTS

The size of the ceiling joists is determined by the span and the weight it must support. The spacing of the ceiling joists is also a factor in determining the size. The section drawing in a set of working drawings will specify the size of the ceiling joists and other wood members to be used. A garage ceiling joist is usually a two by six or a two by eight, spaced 16 inches on center. Always use the size specified in the plans. See Fig. 3-13.

CUTTING CEILING JOISTS

After looking at a set of working drawings, you can see that the ceiling joists are flush with the double wall plate, and are cut with the same pitch as the rafters.

The roof pitch, or slope of the roof, is always specified in

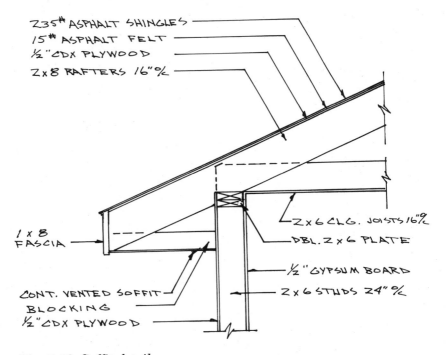

Fig. 3-13. Soffit detail.

the construction plans. If the roof has a $^5/_{12}$ pitch, it means that for every horizontal 12 inches, the roof rises five inches.

The slope of the rafters can be cut on the ceiling joists in one of two ways. They can be measured and cut on the ground before they are put in place, or they can be put in place with square ends and then, line up the cuts with a string. This is done by locating the joist cuts at each end of the garage. Stretch a string between them to locate all of the cuts on the intermediate joists.

NAILING THE CEILING JOISTS

Starting at either end of the garage, position the ceiling joists 16 inches on center. Toenail the joists into the double plate with three 10d nails. To keep the joists vertical, nail temporary one-inch by six-inch bracing across the top of the joists. If flooring is not installed over the ceiling joists, the bracing can be left in place.

4

Roof Construction

THE HEIGHT OF THE ROOF RIDGE IS DETERMINED BY THE SPAN and the pitch of the roof. If the roof has a span of 26 feet and a pitch of $5/12$, the height of the ridge is 65 inches, or 5 feet, 5 inches. To arrive at this figure, divide the span, 26 feet, by 2 and then multiply by 5. The answer is the ridge height.

RAISING THE RIDGE

Using a two by four stud as bracing, secure the ridge at each end of the garage. See Illustration 4-1. Check to make sure that the ridge height at each end is correct.

Brace the center of the ridge with a two by four wood member, then level it with a spirit level.

To check the level of the ridge, attach a string two inches from the top of the ridge at each end. To do this, nail a block of wood at each end of the ridge, then nail the string flush to the block of wood.

Stretch the string taut and then measure between the string and the top of the ridge. The distance between them should be constant.

RAFTER CUTS

After the ridge is level, obtain rafter dimensions from the working drawings and cut a set of rafters for one end of the

Illustration 4-1. *Erecting ridge and rafters.*

structure. Position the rafters in place to make sure they fit. Use the first set of rafters as a guide to cutting the other rafters where they meet the wall plate. To cut the overhang, wait until all of the rafters are in place, and then use the same string method that is used to cut ceiling joists.

RIDGE CUT

The cut for the ridge is marked by aligning a framing square with the foot mark on the arm and the rise per foot on the tongue. See Fig. 4-1.

BIRD'S MOUTH

The bottom of the rafters bear on the inside of the double wall plate. At that point, a bird's mouth cut is notched before the rafters continue beyond the plate to form the overhang.

To cut the bird's mouth, align the inside of the tongue of the carpenter's square with the point that represents the build-

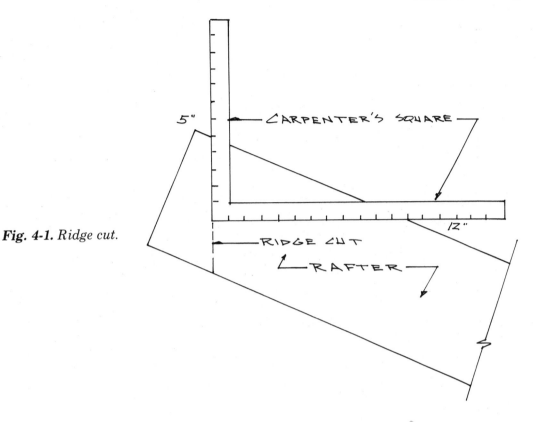

Fig. 4-1. Ridge cut.

ing line. Keep the five and 12-inch marks against the lower edge of the board. See Fig. 4-2.

LAYOUT METHOD

If you have never used a framing square, there is another method that can be used to cut rafters. Lay a pair of rafters on the floor slab and then snap a chalk line to represent the bottom of the rafters and the plate line. Use the rise in 12 inches to establish the proper pitch. Use these as patterns for the other rafters. See Fig. 4-3.

RAFTER MEASURING

One way of obtaining the proper pitch and length of a rafter is to measure the feet by moving the framing square along the rafter and marking it. When the point that represents the

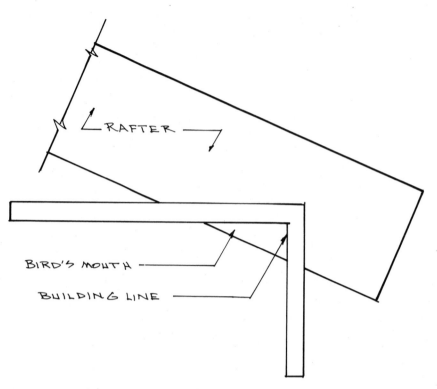

Fig. 4-2. *Bird's mouth cut.*

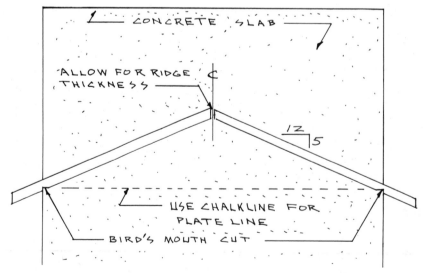

Fig. 4-3. *Rafter layout on floor slab.*

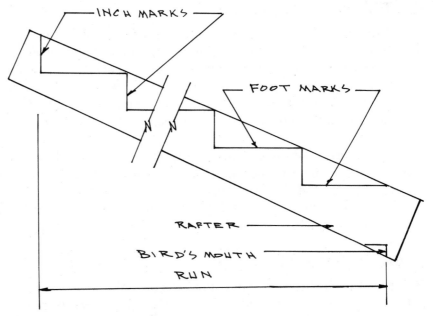

Fig. 4-4. *Rafter measuring.*

building line is reached, turn the square over and align the inside of the tongue with that point, keeping the five and 12-inch marks against the lower edge of the board. See Fig. 4-4. For an overhang, mark the rafter as shown in Fig. 4-5.

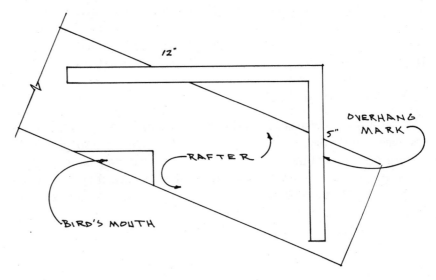

Fig. 4-5. *Overhang cut.*

RAFTER ATTACHMENT

Toenail the rafters to the plate with four 10d nails. The rafters should also be nailed to the ceiling joists. The roof pitch will determine the size and number of nails needed.

Secure a pair of rafters at each end of the garage, then secure another in the middle. The remaining rafters should be positioned directly over the studs, spaced at 16 inches on center.

Add collar ties before removing the bracing. The collar ties are usually one by six wood members spaced 32 inches on center. They should be $1/3$ of the span.

The rafter ends can be trimmed accordingly to accommodate the overhang desired.

SHEATHING INSTALLATION

The roof sheathing should be exterior grade plywood. To determine the proper thickness, check your local building codes. The sheathing should be flush with the rafter edges. After the one by eight fascia board is installed it will butt against the edge of the sheathing, while being flush with the top of the sheathing. The four by eight sheets of exterior plywood sheathing must be staggered. Leave $1/8$-inch space between the panels to allow for expansion.

With the fascia in place, start placing sheathing on a bottom corner of the roof. After the first sheet is nailed, check to make sure that the plywood is flush with the rafter ends, and the gable end is plumb before additional nails are added.

ROOF UNDERLAYMENT

Lay 15-pound asphalt felt over the plywood. Start laying the felt at the eave and overlap each piece by two inches. Only use rough nails to secure the felt until the shingles are in place. One layer of felt is to be laid over the ridge, overlapping the ends by six inches. End laps should be positioned in succeeding courses a minimum of four inches from end laps in preceeding courses. See Fig. 4-6.

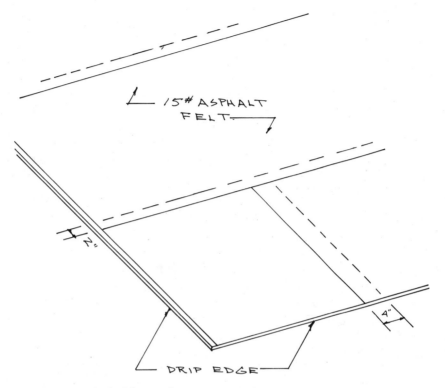

Fig. 4-6. *Asphalt felt overlaps.*

CHALK LINES

The chalk lines positioned on roofing felt act as guide lines to ensure the proper application of the roofing shingles. To obtain horizontal chalk lines, which will be parallel to the eaves, measure the necessary distance on the roof and make a mark. Repeat this process in the middle and at the end. Then position a nail at the mark at each end. Stretch the chalk line between the nails and snap it. The chalk line should be in alignment with the middle mark.

SHINGLES

The two most commonly used shingles are the asphalt shingle and the fiberglass shingle. See Fig. 4-7.

The asphalt shingle has a asphalt-saturated base with a

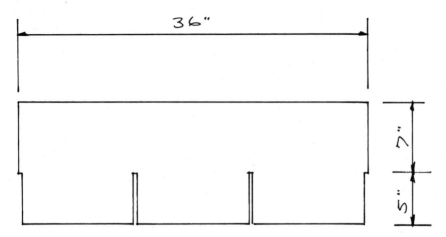

Fig. 4-7. Shingle measurements.

coating of weatherproofing asphalt. This is covered with colored ceramic granules, which protect the asphalt from the sun's rays. These shingles have a sealant strip that bonds the shingles to the surface beneath when the sun's heat acts on the adhesive. Because of this bonding, the shingles stay in place during heavy winds.

The fiberglass shingle is similiar to the asphalt shingle, except that fiberglass replaces the organic felt base of the asphalt shingle. The fiberglass mat, used in fiberglass shingles, is stronger than the organic felt used in asphalt shingles. The fiberglass shingles absorb less moisture, are lighter, and easier to handle and install.

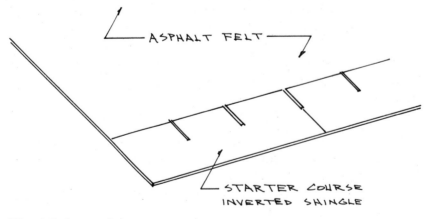

Fig. 4-8. Inverted starter course.

44

SHINGLE INSTALLATION

The starter strip should consist of inverted shingles. See Fig. 4-8. Cut three inches off the rake end of the first shingle, then place a row of inverted shingles along the edge. Take care in the placement of nails, so they will not be exposed by the opening of the first course.

Illustrated by Rick Lamarre

Illustration 4-2. *Applying shingles.*

To lay the first course of shingles, position a full shingle directly on top of the starter strip. Allow the first course of roof shingles to project one inch beyond the edge of the sheathing. To prepare it for nailing, line it up with the rake and soffit edges. Use four galvanized roofing nails on each full shingle.

Start the second course with a full strip minus 1/2 tab. See Illustration 4-2. Start the third course with a full shingle minus the first tab. See Fig. 4-9.

TRUSSES

Trusses are designed to span the full width of the structure. See Fig. 4-10 and Fig. 4-11. Therefore, load-bearing interior partitions are unnecessary. Space the pitch of the roof and the length of the span to determine what size wood members to use to construct trusses. It is recommended that trusses be preengineered by a qualified truss builder. If you are going to use trusses, check your local building codes to determine if you can

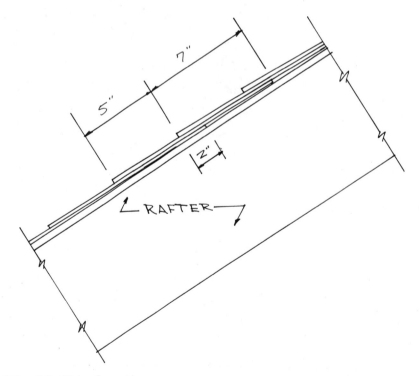

Fig. 4-9. *Shingle section.*

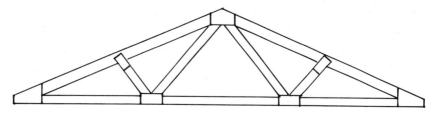

Fig. 4-10. *Roof truss.*

build them on the job site or if they must be pre-engineered by a truss manufacturer.

INSULATION

Because of the high cost of fuel, many homeowners understand the need to increase energy efficiency. There are many insulation products on the market today that are dependable and durable.

The R-value denoted on insulation represents its insulating power. The higher the R-value, the greater the insulating power. For those of you who are struggling with the spiraling high cost of energy, it is recommended that you upgrade the R-value of attic insulation for extra thermal protection. Placing R-38 or R-30 insulation in the attic will improve thermal efficiency and reap considerable economic benefits. See Illustration 4-3. A properly insulated home will provide year-round comfort. If 2 × 4 studs are used on exterior walls, R-13 insulation in the stud wall would be a cost efficient way to improve thermal efficiency. R-19 insulation placed in a 2 × 6 exterior stud wall will provide greater thermal efficiency. Check your local building codes to determine the proper R-value required.

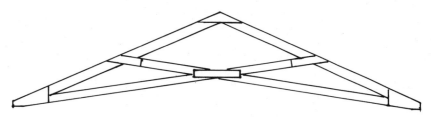

Fig. 4-11. *Scissor trusses create a cathedral ceiling effect.*

Illustration 4-3. *Installing ceiling insulation.*

Illustrated by Rick Lamarre

VENTILATION

The attic space between the ceiling and the roof should be provided with cross ventilation, which should be protected against the entrance of snow and rain. The total net area of vents should be not less than $1/150$ of the ceiling area. It can be $1/300$ if a vapor barrier is installed in the ceiling, or if 50 percent of the required vents are located 3 feet or more above the eave vents, which make up the remainder of the required vent area.

Ventilation alone can effectively control condensation in the attic if the ceiling below is not insulated, provided there is an adequate amount, proper location, continuous operation and free circulation. When insulation is added, ventilation alone is not as effective, and vapor barriers are recommended.

RIDGE VENTS

Continuous ridge vents, if used in conjunction with soffit vents, provide a continuous air flow along the underside of the roof in the attic area. This air flow eliminates moisture that condenses on the roof's cold surface in the winter. In the summer, continuous ridge vents prevent heat from building up by preventing excessive heat from radiating from the roof to the ceiling insulation.

This type of ventilation system protects the insulation, shingles, ceiling, paint, and structural members from moisture problems. In addition, it reduces energy costs, while maintaining summer comfort. It also keeps the roof at an even cold temperature in winter.

5

Siding

IF YOU'D LIKE TO SAVE A SUBSTANTIAL AMOUNT OF MONEY, CONsider applying the siding yourself. The amount of work involved depends on the type of siding you choose. If you plan to use a manufactured siding, consult the manufacturer specifications for proper installation.

BOARD & BATTEN

When applying board and batten siding, space the underboards 1/2 inch apart. Each board should be face-nailed once per bearing. The overlap should not exceed 1 inch. You will need to use nailing blocks between studs. Nail the underboards with 8d nails, and the battens with 8d or 10d nails. See Fig. 5-1.

BOARD ON BOARD

The underboards are to be face-nailed once per bearing, while the overboards are face-nailed twice. The minimum overlap is 1 inch. It is essential to use nailing blocks between studs. This type of siding is applied vertically, using 8d nails for the underboards, and 10d nails for the overboards.

TONGUE AND GROOVE

Most board sidings can be applied horizontally or vertically, but tongue and groove siding can be applied horizontally, vertically, or diagonally. Board siding that locks together, such as tongue and groove siding and shiplap siding,

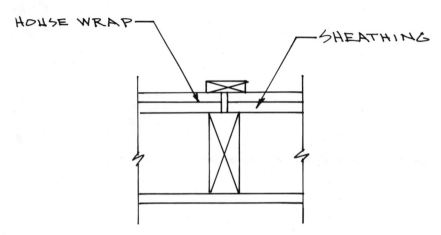

Fig. 5-1. *Board and batten joint.*

can provide more protection and is easier to apply because it aligns with each other.

To apply tongue and groove siding, blind-nail 4 to 6-inch widths through the tongue with 8d finish nails, once per bearing. Face-nail wider boards with two siding nails per bearing. For vertical application, use nailing blocks.

SHIPLAP

For 6-inch widths, face-nail once per bearing. For wider styles, face-nail twice, about 1 inch from overlapping edges. Use 8d nails for 1-inch thickness and 6d nails for thinner boards. Shiplap siding can be applied vertically, or horizontally. If necessary, use nailing blocks over open studs for vertical application.

LAP SIDING

A starter strip $1\frac{1}{2}$-inch wide and $\frac{7}{16}$-inch thick can overlap the foundation wall by 1 inch. Lapsiding can overlap to $1\frac{1}{2}$-inch elsewhere. Nails must penetrate $1\frac{1}{2}$ inches into framing. See Fig. 5-2. Nail $\frac{3}{8}$ inch from the edge on vertical joints. Leave $\frac{1}{8}$-inch gap at doors, windows and corner joints, and caulk.

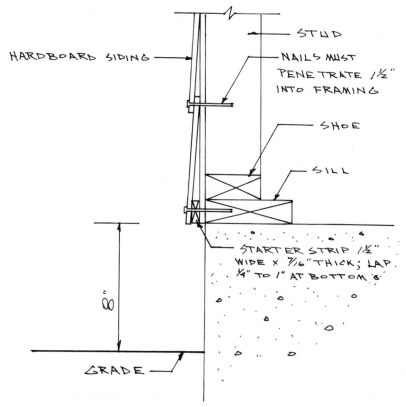

Fig. 5-2. A suggested nailing method for lap siding.

PLYWOOD SIDING

Plywood panels can be applied vertically or horizontally. If applied horizontally, stagger the vertical edge joints and nail the horizontal edges, which join 4 feet up from the base, into firestops or other nailing blocks. Panel edges are to be kept on the center of studs and nailing members.

Nails should be placed every six inches along edges and every 12 inches on intermediate supports. Nail sizes will differ with panel thickness.

Plywood must keep moisture and weather out. Therefore, seal all edges with a water-repellant preservative or a prime coat of paint. Allow 1/16-inch space between panel ends and edge joints for expansion.

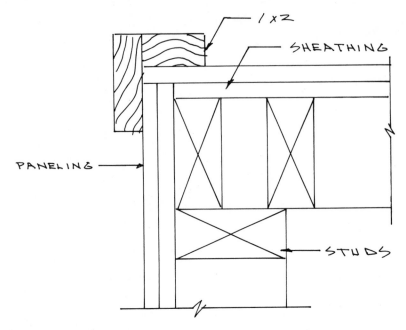

Fig. 5-3. *Corner treatment.*

CORNER BOARDS

Nail ⁵/₄- × -3-inch and a ⁵/₄- × 4-inch corner board the full height of each corner. Position the corner boards 1 inch below the top of the foundation wall. See Fig. 5-3.

6

Installing
Paneling

IF YOU ARE GOING TO CUT THE WALL PANELING WITH A HAND
saw or a table saw, make sure the face of the panel is up to
ensure a smooth cut. If you will be using a portable power cir-
cular saw for cutting, make sure the face of the panel is down.
Support the full panel when cutting and be careful of the panel
edges. Whenever possible, the cut out panels should join in the
middle over doors and windows. Accurate cutting for outlet
boxes and other obstructions is a must. After a panel has been
cut to fit, an ideal way to measure outlet boxes and other obstructions is to mark the obstruction with chalk. When the
panel is placed against the wall, tap it in the obstruction location to transfer the image to the back of the panel, thereby
indicating the area to be cut. The area to be cut should be $1/4$
inch larger to allow for spacing and adjustments.

PANEL EQUALIZING

Before installing wall panels, let them stand for 48 hours
in the area where they will be installed. Stand them up indi-
vidually on their long ends so that both ends are exposed to the
air. This allows the room air to circulate around each panel,
equalizing them to existing humidity conditions.

PANEL FITTING

Start fitting the panels from one corner of the room, allowing 1/4-inch clearance at the top and bottom of each panel. When positioning the first panel, butt it to the adjacent wall. Then plumb it and make sure that the left and right edges of the panel fall on the stud backing. If necessary, trim the outer edge of the panel so that it falls on a stud for nailing.

SPACING THE PANELS

The panels should not touch at the joints. Leave a space equal to the thickness of a coin between the panels and next to doors and window. Before installing the paneling, paint a stripe on the gypsum board between the joints so that it blends with the color of the panel grooves and prevents the wall color from showing through.

TOOLS AND MATERIALS NEEDED

When installing gypsum board wall paneling, the following tools and materials will be needed; gypsum board panels, joint compound, reinforcing tape, corner bead, panel adhesive, annular–ring wallboard nails, wallboard T square, utility knife, metal tape measure, marking pencil, carpenter's hammer, screw gun, keyhole saw or utility saw, joint-finishing knives, a couple of containers for mixing powder joint compounds, mixing paddle, #80 or #100 open-grit sandpaper, a sponge and a respirator.

APPLYING ADHESIVE

Use a good quality panel adhesive to install the wall panels. A water-based adhesive or contact cement is not recommended. Use a caulking gun to apply beads of adhesive in a continuous strip from the top to the bottom and along the four edges of the panels. Nail the corners to hold the panel in place and to let the adhesive set. Consult the manufacturer's instructions before beginning installation.

GYPSUM BOARD PANELS

Gypsum board, which is available in sheet form, is composed of a non-combustible gypsum core encased in a heavy, natural finish paper on the face side. It is available in thicknesses of ½ inch and ⅝ inch and in lengths of 8 to 14 feet. Proper planning will result in smooth interior surfaces. Gypsum board can be applied horizontally or vertically.

PANEL FASTENING

If the gypsum board will be nailed, use ½ inch annular-ring nails for ½-inch thick panel and 1 ⅜-inch annular-ring nails for ⅝-inch thick panels. The nails should be positioned ⅜ of an inch from the ends and edges, spaced 8 inches apart on walls and 7 inches on ceilings. Hold the gypsum board tightly against the framing when nailing. Nail the center of the gypsum board panel first and the perimeter last. Leave a little dimple at the nail head when driving nails, which can be filled with joint compound. Do not break the face paper or fracture the core of the panel by countersinking the nails.

Screw Fastening

If you are using screws for panel fastening, space them 12 inches on the ceiling and 16 inches on walls. They should be positioned ⅜ inch from the panel ends and edges.

Adhesive

For better attachment, while using fewer fasteners, use adhesive. Adhesive should be applied using the manufacturer's specifications.

PREPARATION

Prepare the surface before installing gypsum board panels, by checking the framing members for twisted or bowed studs and/or joints. Position the panel, making sure that the side with the natural-colored face is up, then measure and mark the panel size. See Illustration 6-1. Take a straight edge and line it up with the marks. While holding the straight edge firmly

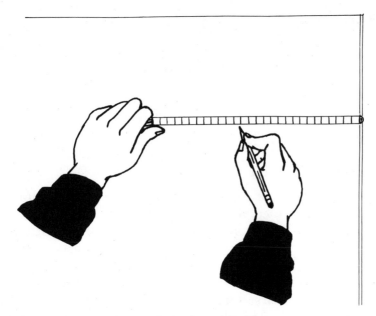

Illustration 6-1. *Measure and mark panel size.*

against the panel, score down through the paper and part of the panel core. See Illustration 6-2. To avoid cutting into the straight edge, hold the knife at a slight angle away from the straight edge. To break the core of the gypsum board panel, snap away from the scored face paper. Run the knife through the back paper to complete the cutting.

Illustration 6-2. *Scoring gypsum board.*

SANDING

Use a rasp or coarse sandpaper wrapped around a block of wood; smooth the cut edges and keep them as square as possible.

CUTOUTS

To cut the openings in panels for fixtures and other obstructions, carefully measure the location and size, then mark them on the gypsum panels. Use a keyhole saw or a utility saw to cut them.

CEILINGS

The ceiling panels should be installed first. If possible, get help to assist handling the gypsum board panels. If help isn't available, and you must do the job yourself, construct some T-braces. These consist of 2 feet lengths of 1 × 4 wood members nailed to 2 × 4 uprights. The T-brace should be ½ inch longer than the floor to ceiling height. Wedge the T-brace between the floor and the ceiling panel, allowing you to apply fasteners to assure firm contact with the ceiling joists. See Illustration 6-3. Starting at the center of the panel and working outward, fasten the panels to the ceiling joists and the perimeter framing. If nails are used, space them 7 inches apart. Space screws 12 inches apart.

WALLS

If the gypsum board wall panels are to be installed horizontally, position the top panel first, snug against the ceiling panels. The end-joints in adjacent rows should be staggered. Install them vertically if the ceiling height is over 8 feet 2 inches, or if the vertical application results in less waste.

Cut the panels to the proper size, so that they don't have to be forced into place. Tapered or wrapped edges should be positioned next to each other. Fasten the panels to the studs and the perimeter framing. If nails are used, space them 8 inches apart.

Illustration 6-3. *Applying ceiling panels with a T-brace.*

COMPOUND APPLICATION

Before using joint compound, place it in a warm room for 24 hours. It should be protected from freezing and kept free from contamination of other joint compounds. If you are going to use the powder-type compound, mix it according to the manufacturer's specifications, using tap water.

JOINT FINISHING

Put a large portion of joint compound across the joint. With a drawing knife, level the compound with the surface of the channel formed by the tapered edges of the gypsum board. Hold the knife at a 45 degree angle in the direction of the joint. After the joint compound is in place, with no bare spots, center reinforcing tape over the joining and, with a joint-finishing knife, press it firmly into the compound. Remove excess compound, but leave enough for a strong bond. Apply a thin layer of compound over the tape to fill the taper flush with the surface of the panels (then allow it to dry). See Illustration 6-4.

END JOINTS

To finish end joints, which are not paper wrapped, center the compound and the tape over the joints. The tape should not overlap when applied at tapered joints. Before applying a second coat, let the taping coat dry for 24 hours. Then with sandpaper or a moistened sponge, level the surface. When applying the second coat, extend the compound 2 inches beyond the taping coat. The edges of the compound should be feathered flush with the face of the panel by applying pressure to the edge of the knife riding the panel. After allowing it to dry, apply a third coat using the same procedure.

INSIDE CORNER FINISHING

On both sides of an inside corner, butter joint compound with a joint-finishing knife. The compound should be extended beyond the area to be covered with tape. Along the center crease, fold the tape and press it into position with your hand. The tape should be firmly seated at the beginning of the joint

Illustration 6-4. *Applying gypsum board.*

Illustrated by Rick Lamarre

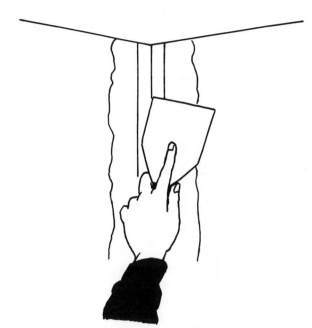

Illustration 6-5. *Finishing an inside corner.*

by wiping each side of the tape flange. Secure the balance of the tape by alternately wiping the excess compound from each side of the joint with a finishing knife, held at a 45 degree angle to the board surface. See Illustration 6-5. Leave enough compound under the tape for a strong bond.

Allow the compound to dry for a minimum of 24 hours before applying a second coat. Cover one side at a time. Allow the first side to dry before applying compound to the second side. The compound should be feathered out onto the face of the panels beyond the first coat. When applying the third coat, the compound should be feathered 2 inches beyond the second coat. After it is dry, sand lightly and remove dust with a damp cloth.

FINISHING OUTSIDE CORNERS

Using a joint-finishing knife, spread enough compound onto the flanges at one end of the corner bead to fill approximately 2 feet of bead at one time. To level the bead, one edge of the knife should ride on the nose of the bead, while the other edge is on the surface of the board.

Flange should be completely filled with compound and extend onto the surface of the panel for a minimum of 4 inches.

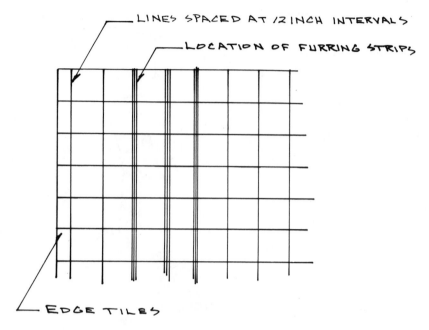

Fig. 6-1. *Make a drawing of your ceiling.*

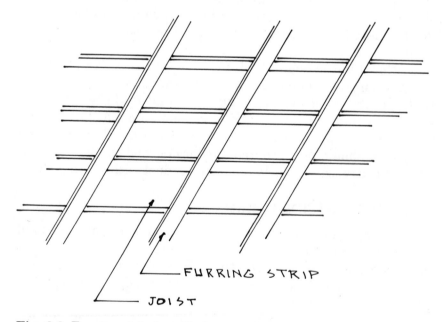

Fig. 6-2. *Furring strip installation.*

Let it dry for 24 hours. After the second coat is applied, let it dry also, then sand lightly. The third coat should be feathered onto the face of the board beyond the second coat. Allow it to dry and then sand dry.

ACOUSTICAL CEILING INSTALLATION

Before purchasing ceiling tile and materials for your acoustical ceiling, make a drawing of your ceiling, denoting the location of ceiling joists and obstructions. Space lines at 12 inch intervals to indicate the number of furring strips you will need. At the same time, you will be able to compute the size of tiles at the edges of the room. Because each ceiling tile is 12 inches

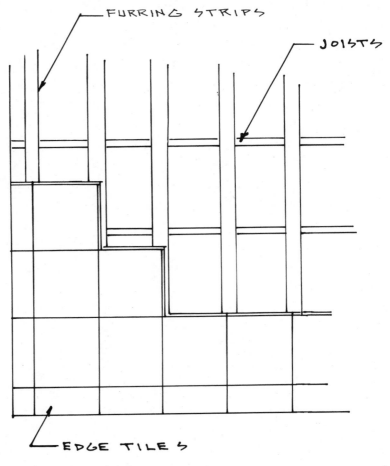

Fig. 6-3. *Ceiling tile placement.*

square, it is a simple matter to determine the number of tiles needed to complete the job. Purchase a few extra tiles in case some accidentally get damaged. See Fig. 6-1.

Nail the tile on by using furring strips, perpendicular to the bottom of the joists. Position the first furring strip at the center of the room. Place the rest of the strips 12 inches apart from center-to-center. The strips should be even. If necessary, shim with thin wedges of wood. See Fig. 6-2. At one end of the room, snap a chalk line down the center of the first furring strip to keep the first row straight.

In the corner of each tile, drive two staples, one directly on top of another. The first staple will cause the legs of the second staple to flare. This method provides a better hold. It might be necessary to glue the final row in place. See Fig. 6-3.

7

Flooring

To install flooring with a minimum amount of time, money, and materials, it is essential to indulge in proper planning and estimating. To estimate the amount of material needed, a sketch on graph paper would be helpful. Record all of the floor dimensions on the sketch. If you have difficulty figuring the amount of flooring needed for each room, a flooring dealer should be able to help you determine the amount and type of flooring needed.

Because carpet and sheet flooring are priced by the square yard, the square footage of the area to be covered has to be divided by nine to obtain the square yardage figures. Tile, however, is priced on a square footage basis.

Before laying flooring, make sure that the sub floor is firm. If it is not, it must be made firm. It is essential that the floor be firm, clean, and even before resilient flooring is installed. A resilient floor is flexible and therefore tends to take the shape of the sub floor.

TOOLS NEEDED

When installing sheet flooring, you will need the following tools and materials:

1. Tape measure for taking measurements

2. Building paper for making patterns

3. Utility knife for cutting sheet flooring

4. Metal straight edge for guiding the utility knife

5. Roller for pressing the flooring to the adhesive

6. Adhesive

7. Sheet flooring

8. Seam sealing compound, if needed

PATTERNS

In rooms that require a sheet of flooring and/or in areas that have obstructions, use patterns as a cutting guide.

1. With building paper, cover the area where sheet flooring is to be installed. If necessary, tape sections of the paper together to obtain the required size.
2. Allow a 1/8-inch gap between the pattern and the wall.
3. Cut the pattern to fit snugly around obstructions and places that will not be covered by baseboards or moulding.
4. With the design facing upward, unroll the sheet flooring.
5. Position the pattern of the flooring at the location you desire and secure it in its proper place.
6. With the pattern as a guide, use a utility knife to make cut outs for the obstructions. Use a metal straight edge with the utility knife to make straight cuts. All cuts should be made in the same direction and be firm enough to penetrate through the flooring with one stroke.

CUTTING FLOORING WITHOUT A PATTERN

If there are no obstructions in the area to be covered, the sheet flooring can be cut without a pattern.

1. Unroll the flooring (outside of the area to be covered) with the design facing up.

2. Measure the area to be covered and record the dimensions.

3. With a utility knife and a straight edge, cut the sheet flooring to oversize measurements of the floor. See Illustration 7-1.

Illustration 7-1. *Cutting vinyl flooring.*

4. Place the oversized sheet into position; allow the excess material to bend up the wall.

5. Press the sheet firmly into the base of the wall. Trim excess material with a utility knife and straight edge, but leave an $1/8$-inch gap for the expansion of walls and floors.

INSTALLING SHEET FLOORING

Vinyl flooring is readily available in 12-foot widths, therefore it is possible to install vinyl flooring with one sheet, which has been cut at the appropiate length. See Illustration 7-2. If more than one sheet of flooring is required, it is best to position each sheet in order to minimize the number of seams. Try to position each sheet so that the seams will not be located in a heavy traffic area.

1. Place the sheet in position. Leave a $1/8$-inch gap along the walls.
2. Roll up half the sheet of flooring.
3. Apply adhesive to the uncovered half of the floor. Check

Illustration 7-2. *Installing vinyl flooring.*

with the manufacturer specifications for the proper method of adhesive application.

4. Roll flooring over the adhesive, while maintaining 1/8-gap along the walls.
5. Apply pressure firmly over the entire surface with a roller. Work the roller from the center to the outer edges, to remove any trapped air.
6. Wipe up excess adhesive with a damp cloth.
7. Repeat steps two through six to lay the second half of the flooring.

SEAMS

When more than one sheet is to be laid, install successive sheets with an overlap, which is later double-cut in order to make a tightly fitting seam.

1. Lay the first sheet as previously explained. Apply adhesive no closer than 6 to 8 inches from the overlap area.

There cannot be any adhesive under the seam when cutting.

2. Lay the remaining sheets, overlapping approximately 1/4 inch. If the design of the flooring requires matching, increase the overlap accordingly.

3. With a utility knife and a straight edge, cut through the overlap. Use firm cutting strokes to cut through two layers of overlap.

4. When the cut is complete, remove the strips from both sheets.

5. Fold back the edges of the sheet flooring, and apply adhesive to the floor along the seam. Do not use excessive amounts of adhesive. This will prevent seepage when the seams are rolled.

6. Firmly place the edges of the sheet flooring into the adhesive.

7. Apply pressure firmly over the seam with a roller.

8. Repeat steps two through seven for the remaining seams.

INSTALLING VINYL MOULDING

Vinyl moulding is easy to handle, easy to install and is a good way to complete your floor.

The adhesive that is used to install flooring is not recommended for vertical surface application. Check with the adhesive manufacturer to determine the proper application of the adhesive. Apply the adhesive in even coats along the base of the wall. Allow it to set according to the manufacturer specifications.

Begin installing vinyl moulding at an inside corner. The molding should be butted tightly against each other and positioned against the wall and floor. Keep a damp rag available for wiping up excess adhesive.

The moulding on the inside corner can be cut to fit by mitering the ends of the sections with a utility knife.

TILE FLOORS

In order to lay tile properly on floors, it is important to snap chalk lines that can be used as a guide to putting tiles squarely in place. To do this, locate the center of the two side walls and place a mark on the floor at each center. Attach a chalk line to one mark and pull it to the mark on the opposite wall. Pull the line taut, then pull the line straight up from the floor and release it. The chalk line will leave a straight line on the floor. Repeat the above steps to make a chalk line between the two end walls.

Beginning where the chalk lines intersect, lay two rows of loose tiles perpendicular to each other. See Fig. 7-1. This determines the width of the tiles along the borders. Narrow tiles along the borders of the floor are less desirable than wider tiles.

The chalk lines do not have to be adjusted if the distance between the last tiles and the wall is the width of a half of a tile or more. If the distance is less than the width of a half of a tile, however, the rows must be adjusted and new chalk lines marked on the floor.

Adjust the row until the distance between the last tile and the wall is equal to the width of a half of a tile or more. Then, using the rows as a guide, snap two new chalk lines parallel to

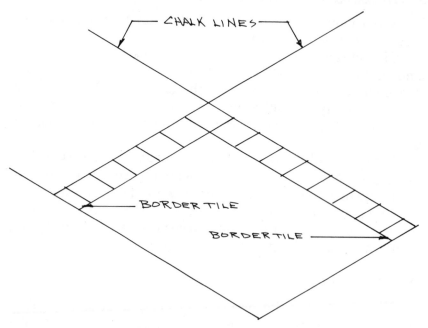

Fig. 7-1. *Squaring off the floor.*

the old ones. The new chalk lines can be used a a guide for positioning tiles.

CUTTING BORDER TILE

When all of the whole tiles have been put in place in a portion of the floor, the border tiles should be measured and cut. To accurately measure and mark a border tile, position a loose tile on top of the last whole tile. Make sure that the edges of the tiles are aligned. The loose tile should be facing up.

Place another tile on top of the loose tile and hold one edge of it firmly against the wall. See Fig. 7-2. Using the edge of the top tile as a guide, mark on the loose tile. After removing the tile from the floor, make a light cut along the mark to guide the utility knife.

With a metal straight edge, firmly held against the mark, cut the tile with a sharp knife. The cut border tile should now fit snugly into place.

INSTALLING TILES

Whole tiles and border tiles are laid in one section at a time before beginning the next section. See Fig. 7-3. Always

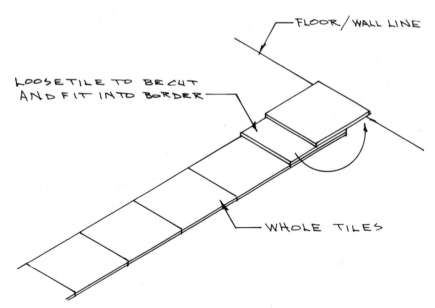

Fig. 7-2. *Cutting border tiles.*

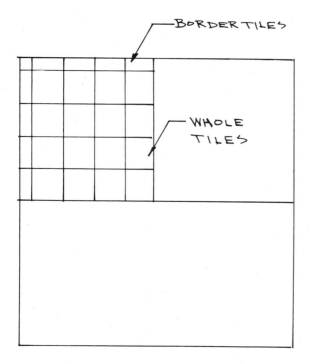

Fig. 7-3. *Tiles are put in place one section at a time.*

begin laying tiles at the section farthest from the entry.

Apply an even coat of adhesive to an entire section. Consult the manufacturer's specifications for proper application.

The first tile should be laid where the chalk line intersect. The other tiles are to be butted firmly against adjacent tiles and should be laid in the sequence as shown.

It is best to put the tiles in their correct position the first time. See Fig. 7-4. Do not attempt to slide the tiles into position. Have a damp rag handy to wipe up excess adhesive.

Cut and lay the border tiles after the whole tiles of a section are laid.

With a roller apply pressure to all the tiles in the section. Repeat this process for laying tiles in the remaining sections. Baseboards can be installed after the entire floor is tiled.

INSTALLING ROLL CARPETING

If you are building living quarters over a garage, most likely one of the rooms will be carpeted. Before installing carpet, make sure that the floor is firm, even, and clean. Check

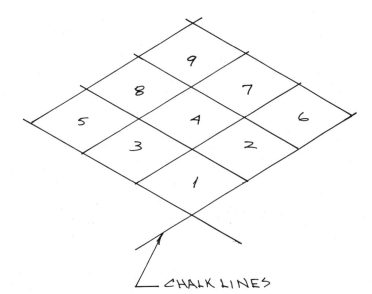

Fig. 7-4. *Tile laying sequence.*

the floor for protruding nails, loose boards, cracks, gaps, and high and low spots. If any of these situations exist, repair them before installing carpet.

The floor plan of a set of working drawings, denotes the dimensions of the room to be covered. With this information you will be able to estimate the materials needed. Determine the number of square feet by multiplying the length by the width of the room. Select a carpet wide enough to eliminate seams. If it is not possible to avoid seams, locate them away from heavy traffic areas.

The carpet is secured at the edges of the room with double-face tape. Binder bars will be necessary to protect the edges of the carpet at doorways. You can determine the amount of molding needed using the perimeter dimensions of the room.

Among the tools needed to install roll carpeting are:

1. Utility knife for cutting the carpet
2. Metal straight edge, which is used to guide the knife
3. Scissors to cut the tape
4. Chalk line to mark the carpet if it is necessary to make seams
5. Double-face tape to secure the carpet
6. Seaming tape, if necessary

Apply double-face tape to the floor but do not remove the protective paper from the top of the tape. Apply the tape at all edges around the room and around obstructions.

Using chalk, mark lines to be cut on the carpet. The carpet should be cut oversized before it is positioned in the room. Allow an extra 2 inches or more at all edges to be fitted. Position the straight edge firmly against the carpet on the line to be cut. With a utility knife, cut along the straight edge with a firm stroke. Place the carpet in the installed position. Before cutting the extra carpet from the edges, press the carpet tightly into the corner where the floor and the wall meet. Cut the carpet at the corner with the utility knife. Fit and cut the remaining edges as required. Once the carpet has been cut to fit, check the fit at all edges and trim as necessary.

Lay the carpet out on the floor and check to see that it fits. Then roll it up to the starting wall. As the carpet is unrolled it must be pulled tightly to prevent wrinkles and bulges. The protective paper should be removed from the tape as the carpet is unrolled. After the carpet is aligned with the end wall, install the shoe molding if desired.

8

Decks, Stairs, Doors and Windows

A COUPLE OF THE GARAGE PLANS IN THIS BOOK HAVE A DECK. Although the decks shown are basic, the design and size can be varied to suit individual needs and desires. Care should be taken, however, to stay within the local building codes.

Stake out the location of the deck with stakes and string similar to the batter board method explained in Chapter 1. The posts that support the deck are supported by concrete piers that are poured below the frost level, as required by code.

The width and height of the deck should be marked on the wall of the structure. From the height mark at each end of the width of the deck, measure the thickness of the deck material to be used and then make a second mark. See Fig. 8-1. Tie a string tightly between the nails at the marks. Adjust the string until it is level. When the string is level, snap a chalk line along the span of the string. The top edge of the ledger board will run along this line. Measure down the height of the joists and make another mark. This mark represents the bottom of the joists and header, and the top of the posts.

The joists are butted against the ledger board and the header with joist hangers. See Fig. 8-2. The size of the joists

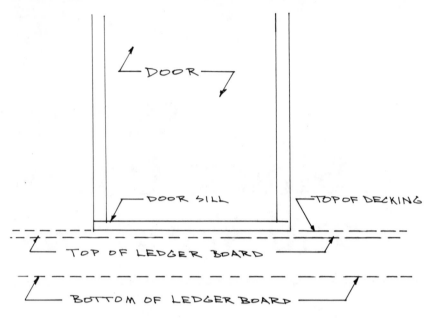

Fig. 8-1. *Chalk line marks.*

and the size of the header are determined by their unsupported span and the weight they must carry. See Fig. 8-3.

Space the decking to allow for water runoff. If the decking is not spaced, pitch the deck away from the structure. See Illustration 8-1.

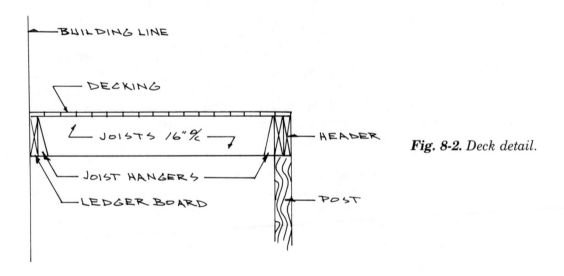

Fig. 8-2. *Deck detail.*

78

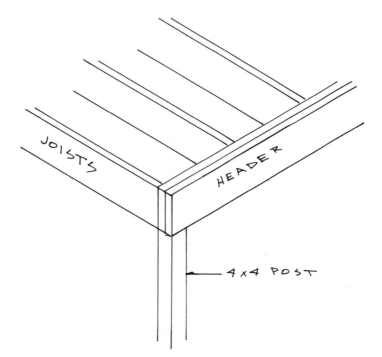

Fig. 8-3. *Head/Post detail.*

STAIRS

Stairs consist of risers, treads, and stringer. Treads are the portion of the stairway that you step on. The riser is the vertical height between each tread, and stringers are 2 × 12 wood members that are notched to receive the treads.

The number of risers and treads in a set of stairs is determined by the floor-to-floor height. To determine the height of each riser, divide the floor-to-floor height by the number of risers. For example, if the floor-to-floor height is 116 inches, you will need 15 risers at 8.28 inches. (115 divided by 15 equals 8.28.) In many areas the maximum riser height is 8.25 inches. Anything higher would be too steep. Therefore, instead of 15 risers, you could use 14 risers at 7.73 inches (116 divided by 14 risers equals 7.73). There is always one more riser than there are treads. The tread width is usually 9 inches. Check your local building codes. If a floor-to-floor height is 116 inches, you will need 14 risers at 7.73 inches and 13 treads at 9 inches.

The run is the horizontal distance the stairs must occupy.

Illustration 8-1. *Building a deck.*

Illustrated by Rick Lamarre

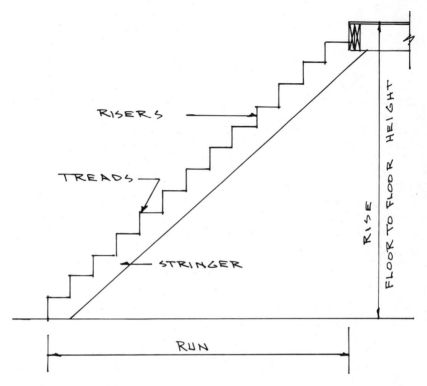

Fig. 8-4. *Stair layout.*

See Fig. 8-4. The run is the sum of the stair treads (13 treads multiplied by 9 inches equals 112 inches).

Stair Layout

On the tongue of a framing square, mark the riser height, then mark the width of the tread on the blade. Lay the square near the top end of the stringer, leaving enough room to cut the end off of the angle that formed by setting each mark on the square directly over the board's edge. Mark the rise and run along the outside of the square with a pencil. Then slide the square along the stringer so that the mark on the tongue is directly over the mark just made along the blade. Repeat this process for each riser and tread on both stringers. See Fig. 8-5.

Cut along the layout lines after the layout is complete. All of the risers should be the same height except the lower one, which is shorter than the others. The tread thickness adds to

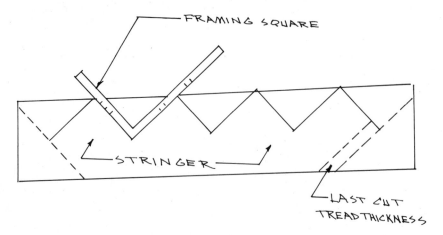

Fig. 8-5. Stringer layout.

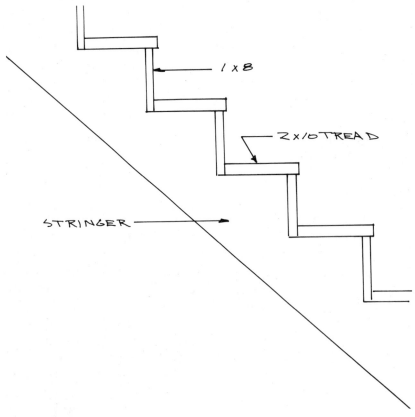

Fig. 8-6. Stair detail.

the first steps height, therefore, to shorten the height of the last step, cut an amount off of the bottom of the stringer to equal the thickness of the tread.

Treads and Risers

For treads, you can use 2 × 10 wood members. Risers can be 1 × 8 wood members, cut to the proper width. Nail risers to the stringer first using 8d finishing nails. See Fig. 8-6. Treads should be nailed to the stringers with 12d finishing nails. Use 8d nails to nail the bottom edges to the back of the treads.

Finally, anchor the stairs securely at the top and bottom.

INSTALLING A DOOR

Today, framing and hanging a door is made easy with factory built, pre-hung door frames. A pre-hung door frame is similar to a rectangle with a door hinged to it. The unit is slipped into the stud frame opening and secured. The pre-hung door frame consist of two side jambs and a head jamb, which are

Fig. 8-7. *Selection of door styles.*

dadoed together at the top. To keep the door from closing too far, a door stop runs around the inside jambs. See Fig. 8-7.

At the base of the two side jambs, a sill and threshold are needed for exterior doors. The sill is milled from one piece of lumber and slopes away from the door's base to keep water away. The threshold closes the opening between the floor and the bottom edge of the door.

Pre-hung door frames purchased from a dealer will have the door and the door stop already attached. Remove the hinge pins, the door stop, and the door before installing the door frame in place.

Framing

The framing plans, which are provided in a set of working drawings, show the rough openings of doors and windows. The size of the header is also denoted. Header size is based on the span and the weight it must carry. The header is supported by two jack studs. The size of the rough opening is determined by the size of the door. See Fig. 3-4. The height of the door is usually 6 feet, 8 inches. Therefore, the height of the rough opening should be 6 feet, 9 inches to allow for the head jamb and $1/2$ inch clearance near the floor.

The rough opening should be square. The door will not work properly if the opening is framed irregular.

The header consist of two wood members on edge, which are separated by $1/2$-inch spacers. Staggered along its length are 12d or 16d nails.

Cut away the shoe, flush with the studs. Avoid cutting in to the finished floor.

Hanging the Door

When hanging a pre-hung door frame in a rough opening, keep the door frame plumb and level at all times. The rough opening is slightly larger than the size of the pre-hung frame. This allows for shimming the frame into exact plumb and level. Shimming is done by driving a pair of shingles together from each side of the frame to form a tight wedge.

Center the pre-hung door frame in the rough opening. At the lower hinge location, begin shimming to the estimated side clearance. Fasten with 10d finishing nails where the door stop will cover.

After shimming, check plumb and then nail halfway between the top and bottom shims, where the door stop will cover. Secure the door into position with the hinge pins. When shimming and nailing the latch side of the door frame, be sure to keep $1/16$ inch clearance between the door edge and the frame. Nail the sill and threshold of an exterior door to the joists at this time. Keep the top of the sill flush with the finished floor level.

Consult the manufacturer's instructions to install a door knob and a striker plate. Starting on the hinge side, nail a length of door stop from the floor to the top of the inside corner of the frame. Use 4d finishing nails every 12 inches. Keep the door stop $1/16$ inch away from the door face on the hinge side to prevent the door from binding, if it is painted.

When installing trim around the frame's edges, use 6d or 8d finishing nails spaced every 16 inches.

INSTALLING WINDOWS

Installing a window is much the same as installing a door. They are sold in pre-hung units that are slipped in to the rough

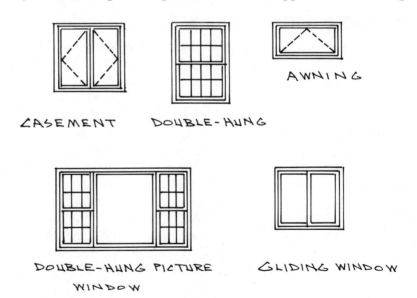

Fig. 8-8. *Selection of window styles.*

opening and then leveled and fastened.

Many sizes and styles of windows are available to choose from. There are double-hung windows, casement windows, sliding windows, awning windows, bow windows, bay windows, and picture windows. See Fig. 8-8.

Wood windows are shimmed into proper level, while aluminum windows are just put into position, leveled, and nailed to the wall framing.

Check with the manufacturer specifications to determine the size of the rough opening. The framing of the rough opening is similar to a door's rough opening. See Fig. 3-3. Before nailing the sill in place, adjust the opening's height and make sure it is square. The sill should be level. Nail cripple studs at each end of the sill and at 16 inches on center for the span of the sill. The rough opening height should be the same as the rough opening height of the doors. When the framing is complete, the window should be hung to manufacturer specifications.

When determining window size for living areas, check your local building codes. Some states have requirements regarding the percentage of window area needed in each room, in addition to egress requirements for bedrooms.

OVERHEAD GARAGE DOORS

The most common garage door is the sectional, upward-acting door. Although wood overhead doors are favored most, they are also available in fiberglass and metal. Window units in overhead doors are optional. See Fig. 8-9. The framing for the overhead door is detailed in the framing plans in a set of construction drawings. The ceiling height of a garage should be high enough to allow for the overhead door track.

The construction of an overhead door consist of horizontal sections that are butted together in tongue and groove, rabbetted, or similar joints. These joints are secured from behind with hinges that allow the sections to flex, enabling the door to roll overhead. There is a track on each side of the door. Hinges on the door edges fit into the tracks, which use rollers that are mounted on the sides of the hinges. Springs attached to the

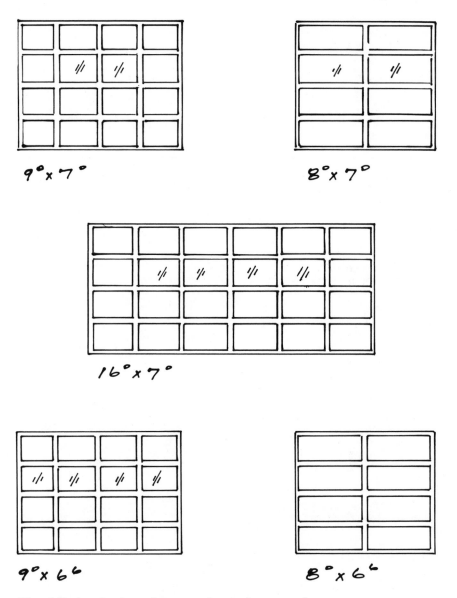

9° x 7°

8° x 7°

16° x 7°

9° x 6⁶

8° x 6⁶

Fig. 8-9. *A selection of commonly used garage doors.*

overhead tracks act as a counter-balance to the door, preventing it from closing too fast when it is closed.

Installing an overhead door can be completed before the interior is finished, thereby enabling you to work inside if the weather is bad.

9

Plumbing and Electrical

T HE PLUMBING SYSTEM FOR THE LIVING QUARTERS BEGIN AT THE water utility's main or at the well if you have a private water system. Once installed, the plumbing will provide all the water you need. It will treat it, heat it, then deliver it to where it is used. Water that isn't consumed must be drained out of the house. All residential plumbing systems consist of three parts: the water supply system, the fixtures, and the drainage system.

WATER SUPPLY SYSTEM

The water supply system is comprised of a service entrance line from the water main to a meter (if you have city water), a main shutoff near the water, a distribution system, and a water heater. The water supply system also usually includes room shutoffs and fixture stop cocks. Some of the fixtures might be used for one kind of water, hot or cold. Cold and hot water branches extend from the main and lead to the fixtures. See Fig. 9-1. Because they only carry enough water for one fixture, the branches are a smaller pipe size than mains. Mains are usually the same size throughout their length. A riser is the part of the main or branches that go up through the walls. The hot water main is usually a continuous loop, which is constantly circulating hot water from the water heater.

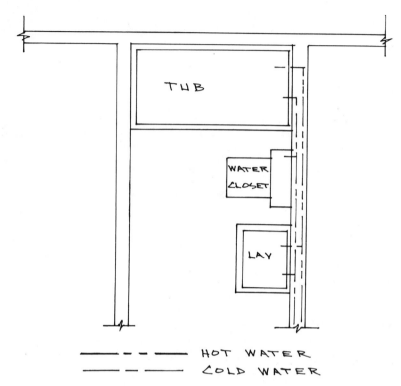

Fig. 9-1. Water supply layout for bathroom.

DRAINAGE SYSTEM

After water is used, it flows out of the fixtures and is carried away by the plumbing. The gases that are created by the decomposition within the system must also be dispelled, so that you won't have to breathe them. This is the purpose of the drainage system. The drainage system consists of pipes that have ample capacity and are properly pitched, which carry wastes away by gravity. The whole system is tightly-sealed and properly vented. In the event that the drain pipes should ever clog, you need to make provisions for how to clean them out.

The soil stack is a large vertical pipe that collects waste from one or more fixtures. See Fig. 9-2. Each fixture is connected to the soil stack by a branch drain, which must slope downward toward the soil stack. The soil stack extends below

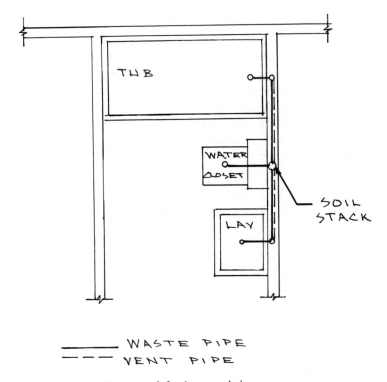

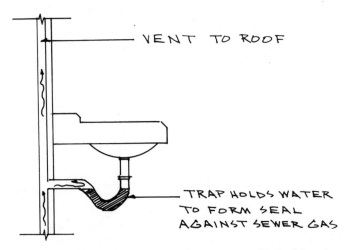

Fig. 9-2. Bathroom layout of drainage piping.

Fig. 9-3. The trap is a U-shaped pipe that is always filled with water.

the house where it connects with a horizontal sloped pipe—the house drain. The house drain leaves the building and enters the ground beyond the foundation where it connects with the city sewer system or private sewage system.

A vent pipe extends through the roof and is located near the soil stack. It is sized accordingly and is used for gases only.

A closet bend is a large pipe that connects the toilet to the soil stack. Every toilet has its own water trap. All other fixtures have separate traps to keep gases from escaping into the house. A trap is a U-shaped pipe—always filled with water—that seals off the drain piping beyond it. See Fig. 9-3.

ELECTRICITY

Supplying electricity to a detached garage involves connecting the interior wiring to an exterior conduit. This connection can be made through the foundation wall or through the frame wall.

Electrical Cable

Be sure to shut off the main power switch before doing any electrical work. Do not attempt to do any electrical work while the electrical power is on. Because this section is about extending wiring from the house, it would be wise to evaluate the existing usage to determine if a new circuit is needed. BX cable is enclosed in a flexible metal casing. It consists of three wires. The black hot wire and the white neutral wire are paper-wrapped. There is also a green ground wire or a bare ground wire. BX is flexible enabling it to turn corners easily. It is also good for use in dry indoor locations.

Figure 9-4 shows the electrical symbols used in the working drawings in this book.

Underground

Before bringing the wire from the inside of the house to the outside, you must decide what type of wire to use and how the circuits will be installed. It is advisable to check your local building codes regarding any specific requirements. Some codes stipulate that outdoor wiring be placed in rigid conduit, from

ELECTRICAL SYMBOLS	
$	SINGLE-POLE SWITCH
$₃	THREE-WAY SWITCH
⊖	DUPLEX OUTLET
⊖R	RANGE OUTLET
○	LIGHTING OUTLET
○GFI	GROUND FAULT INTERRUPTER

Fig. 9-4. *Electrical symbols used on working drawings in this book.*

the point in which it leaves the house, to the spot where it disappears below ground.

Underground wire is usually UF cable, which is designed to be buried in the ground. When wiring emerges from the ground, it is recommended that rigid conduit be used with type TW wires, which have coverings that are moisture resistant.

Eave Entry/Exit

When exiting the wire through an eave, position the assembled outdoor box, corner elbow, section of conduit, and nipple against the soffit. Place the conduit adjacent to the siding and position the box between two rows of nails in the soffit. By using the outdoor box as a template, make a mark on the soffit indicating the location of the cable hole. Make additional marks to indicate the location of holes needed for mounting screws.

After the cable has been pushed through the cable hole from an indoor circuit, fasten it on a two-part connector; then screw the box to the connector. Mount the box on the soffit. Fasten the conduit to the wall. Fasten the nipple to the soffit. As necessary, bend the conduit to run it into the trench.

Trench

You will have to dig a trench to receive the wire exiting from the house. Stake out the trench and make it as straight as possible. It should be about eight inches wide and at least 12 inches deep.

10

Driveways

THE WIDTH OF THE DRIVEWAY CONNECTING THE GARAGE AND the road should be wide enough to suit your needs. A driveway about 9 or 10 feet wide is ideal for a one-car garage. A driveway for a two-car garage, however, should be widened accordingly. When designing a driveway thought should be given to a turnaround area. See Fig. 10-1.

LAYING COLD ASPHALT

Cold asphalt can be purchased premixed and is ideal for the homeowner who intends to spread the asphalt himself.

The surface to be paved with asphalt should be prepared the same way as it should be prepared for concrete. Because the edges of asphalt crumble, special attention should be given to a permanent building form. Cross ties, concrete, stone, or any material can be used for the permanent frame if it is substantial enough to keep the asphalt in place. If wood members are used, they should be pressure-treated and be a minimum of 2 inches thick and 4 to 6 inches wide.

To prepare a base, spread 2 inches of sand evenly over the area to be paved. Place small mounds of the asphalt mix on the area to be paved. Level the mounds with a garden rake then dump out some more mix. Do not do more than a few feet at a time. The asphalt should be raked to a 5-inch thickness. The center of the driveway should be built-up and sloped to the side.

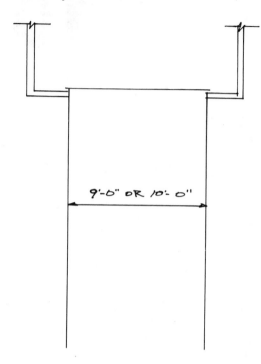

9'-0" OR 10'-0"

Fig. 10-1. *The ideal width for a one-car garage driveway is 9 or 10 feet.*

To obtain a smooth surface, roll and tamp the asphalt with a roller and a tamper. The surface should be rolled until it is smooth and compacted. High areas can be tamped with a asphalt tamper.

CONCRETE DRIVEWAY

The edge of a driveway should be approximately 1 inch below the garage floor. This will prevent water from seeping into the garage. When possible, the driveway should slope downward from the garage.

The top of a driveway is usually two inches above ground level. The driveway should be 4 or 5 inches thick if it will be used for passenger cars.

A sideways pitch of ¼ inch to ½ inch per foot should be given to the entire drive. This can be done by crowning the driveway, providing pitch from the center of the drive to both sides. This is accomplished by pouring the driveway in two stages.

Build the entire form for the driveway. Then center a stopboard lengthwise in the form. It must be high enough to obtain

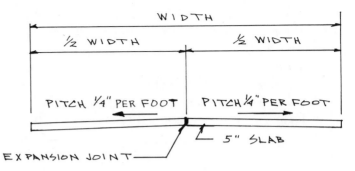

Fig. 10-2. *A cut-away view of a concrete driveway with expansion joint.*

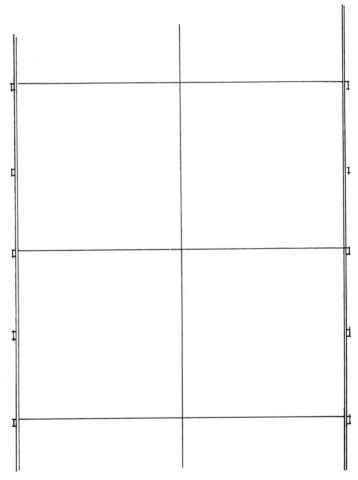

Fig. 10-3. *Concrete poured in sections.*

the desired pitch. Both sides of the slab will be held together with #4 reinforcing rods. These should be 36 inches long and spaced 40 inches apart.

The base of the driveway is usually 4 inches of gravel or crushed stone in addition to 2 inches of sand. After tamping the base material, lay reinforcing mesh on rocks so that it does not touch the forms. Place isolation joints between the driveway and the garage.

Start pouring the slab at the garage and work toward the street or road. If it is a long driveway, break it up into 10-foot sections by installing a stopboard every 10 feet. Pour concrete into the first section and tamp. Screed the concrete and place excess into the next unpoured section. See Fig. 10-2.

Remove the stopboard after the first half of the slab is finished. Then repeat the process for the rest of the driveway. See Fig. 10-3.

11

Garage Building Plans

NATHAN

THE NATHAN IS A ONE-CAR GARAGE WITH DISTINCTIVE ANGLED siding. The triangular louver provides adequate ventilation. The 14 foot width provides ample room for getting in and out of a car.

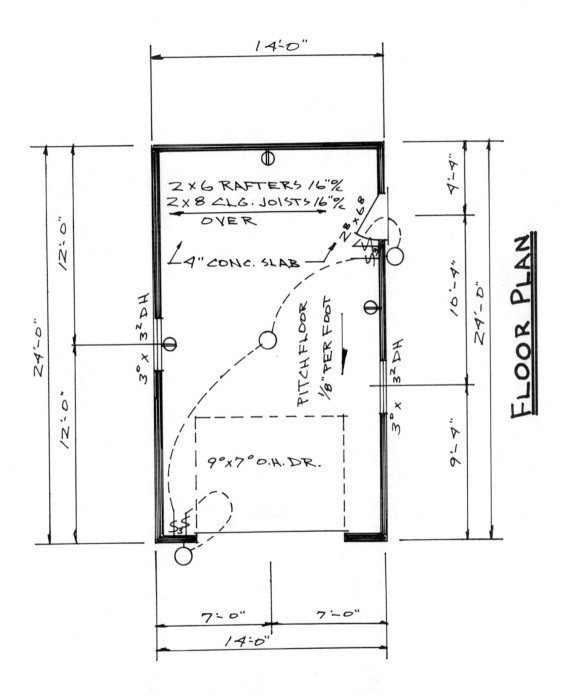

14'-0"

2 × 6 RAFTERS 16"%
2 × 8 CLG. JOISTS 16"%
OVER

4" CONC. SLAB

2⁸ × 6⁸

12'-0"

24'-0"

12'-0"

3⁰ × 3² DH

PITCH FLOOR
⅛" PER FOOT

9⁰ × 7⁰ O.H. DR.

3² DH

3⁰ × 3² DH

4'-4"

16'-4"

24'-0"

9'-4"

FLOOR PLAN

7'-0"   7'-0"

14'-0"

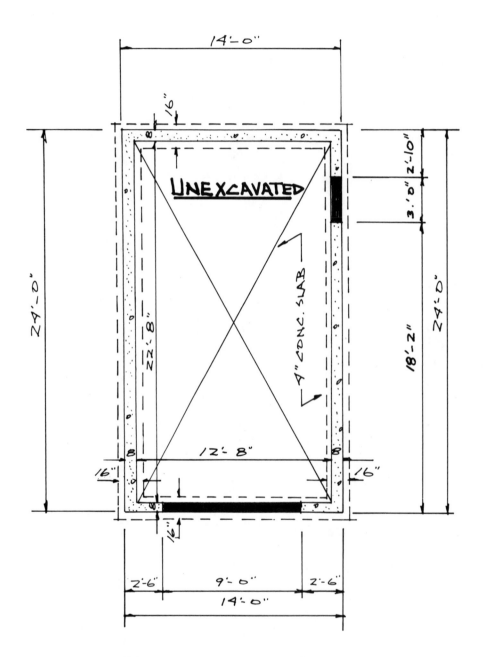

FOUNDATION PLAN

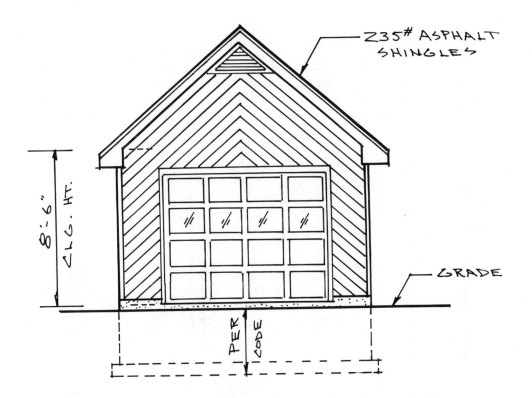

235# ASPHALT SHINGLES

8'-6" CLG. HT.

GRADE

PER CODE

FRONT ELEVATION

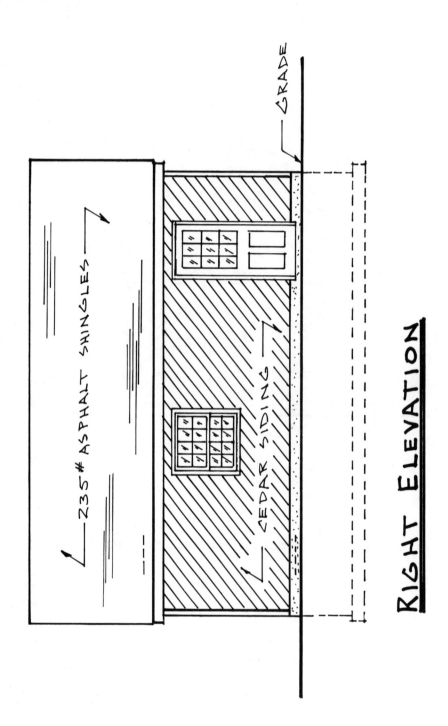

235# ASPHALT SHINGLES

CEDAR SIDING

GRADE

RIGHT ELEVATION

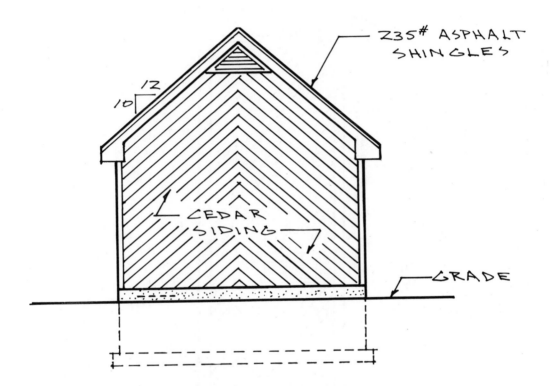

235# ASPHALT SHINGLES

12
10

CEDAR SIDING

GRADE

REAR ELEVATION

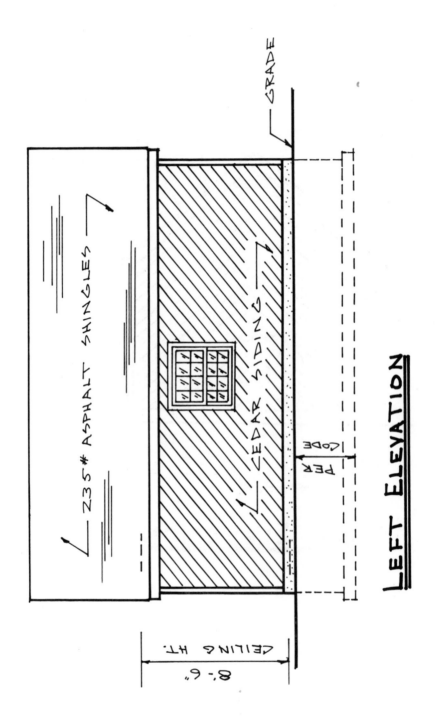

235# ASPHALT SHINGLES

GRADE

CEDAR SIDING

PER CODE

CEILING HT.
8'-6"

LEFT ELEVATION

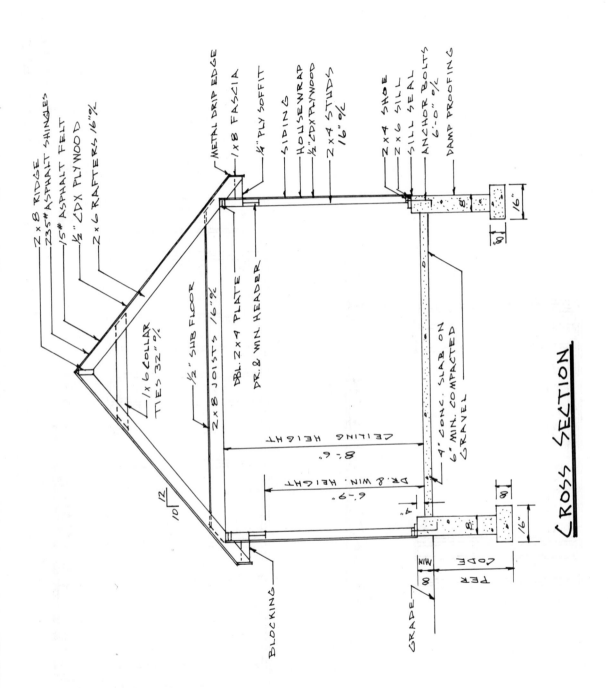

CROSS SECTION

Labels (rotated):
2 x 8 RIDGE
235# ASPHALT SHINGLES
15# ASPHALT FELT
1/2" CDX PLYWOOD
2 x 6 RAFTERS 16" o/c
METAL DRIP EDGE
1 x 8 FASCIA
1/4" PLY SOFFIT
SIDING
HOUSEWRAP
1/2" CDX PLYWOOD
2 x 4 STUDS 16" o/c
2 x 4 SHOE
2 x 6 SILL
SILL SEAL
ANCHOR BOLTS 6'-0" o/c
DAMP PROOFING
1 x 6 COLLAR TIES 32" o/c
1/2" SUB FLOOR
2 x 8 JOISTS 16" o/c
DBL. 2 x 4 PLATE
DR. & WIN. HEADER
CEILING HEIGHT 8'-6"
DR. & WIN. HEIGHT 6'-9"
4" CONC. SLAB ON 6" MIN. COMPACTED GRAVEL
BLOCKING
GRADE
8" MIN
PER CODE
12
10
8"
4"
6"
8"
8"
16"
16"

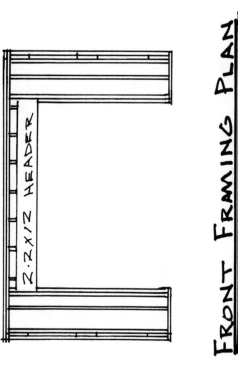

FRONT FRAMING PLAN

2·2x12 HEADER

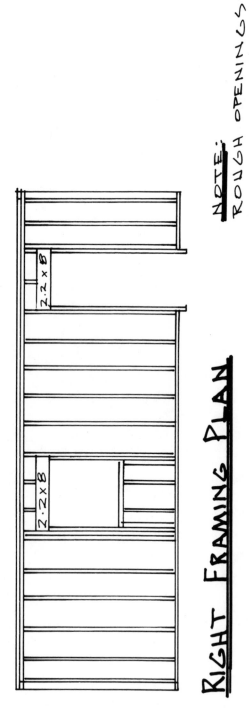

RIGHT FRAMING PLAN

2·2 x B

2·2 x B

NOTE:
ROUGH OPENINGS
BY MANUFACTURER

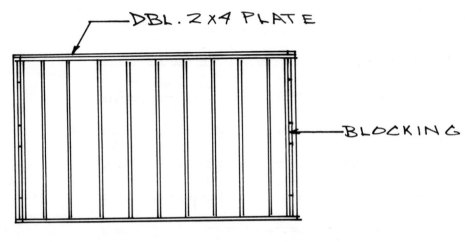

DBL. 2X4 PLATE

BLOCKING

REAR FRAMING PLAN

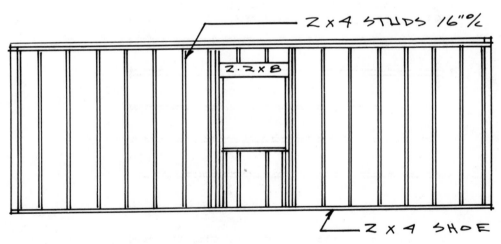

2X4 STUDS 16"%

2·2X8

2X4 SHOE

LEFT FRAMING PLAN

2×8 CLG. JOISTS 16"%

CEILING FRAMING PLAN

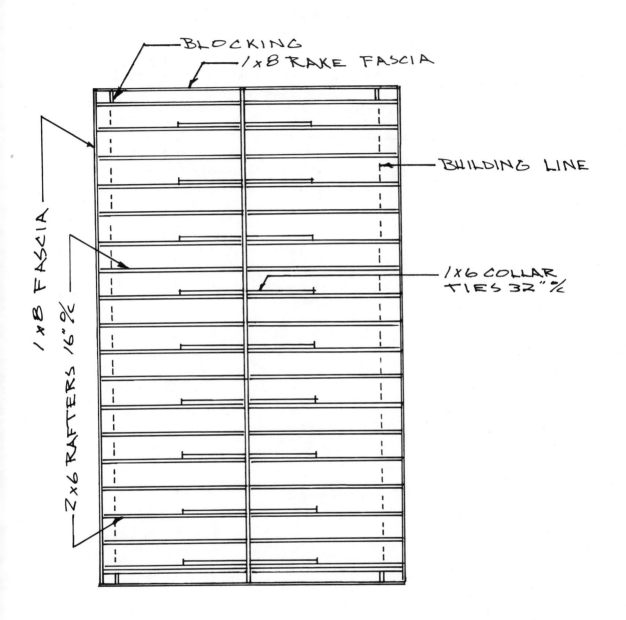

BLOCKING

1x8 RAKE FASCIA

BUILDING LINE

1x6 COLLAR TIES 32" %

1x8 FASCIA

2x6 RAFTERS 16" %

ROOF FRAMING PLAN

MATERIAL LIST
The Nathan

2 × 6 Sill-----2/14---4/12
Sill Seal----------64 lineal feet
Anchor Bolts-------13
2 × 4 Shoe--------2/14---4/12
Dbl. 2 × 4 Plate--4/14---8/12
2 × 4 Studs--------67/8
Door Headers
    2 × 12----2/10
    2 × 8-----1/6

Window Headers
    2 × 8----1/14
½" × 4' × 8' Sheathing----
  17 sheets
Housewrap-------522 square feet

Siding-----------522 square feet
Ceiling Joists-----(2 × 8) 18/14
2 × 8 Ridge--------1/12---1/14
2 × 6 Rafters------38/12
Shingles-----------16 bundles
Asphalt Felt-------2 rolls
½" × 4' × 8' Roof
  Sheathing-----16 sheets
¼" × 12" Soffit----5/10
¼" × 6" Rake Soffit----4/12
1 × 8 Fascia-------5/10
1 × 8 Rake Fascia-----4/12
1 × 6 Collar Ties----9/6
Drip Edge----------5/10

SHAWN

The Shawn is a 22 feet × 22 feet two-car garage. The roof treatment, in addition to the vertical siding, gives it the look of a carriage shed. Casement windows provide natural light on both sides and the rear.

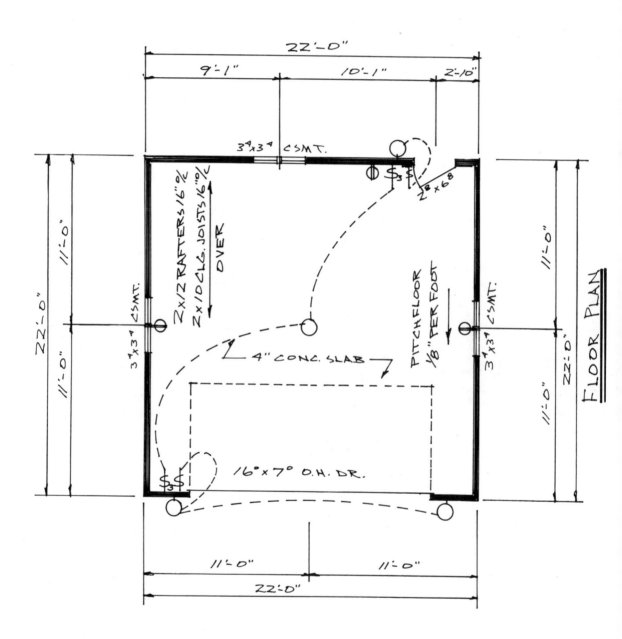

FLOOR PLAN

22'-0"

9'-1"   10'-1"   2'-10"

3"x3" CSMT.

2x12 RAFTERS 16"O/C
2x10 CLG. JOISTS 16"O/C
OVER

2'8"x68"

PITCH FLOOR
1/8" PER FOOT

4" CONC. SLAB

16'0"x7'0" O.H. DR.

3"x3" CSMT.

3"x3" CSMT.

22'-0"

11'-0"

11'-0"

22'-0"

11'-0"

11'-0"

11'-0"

11'-0"

22'-0"

114

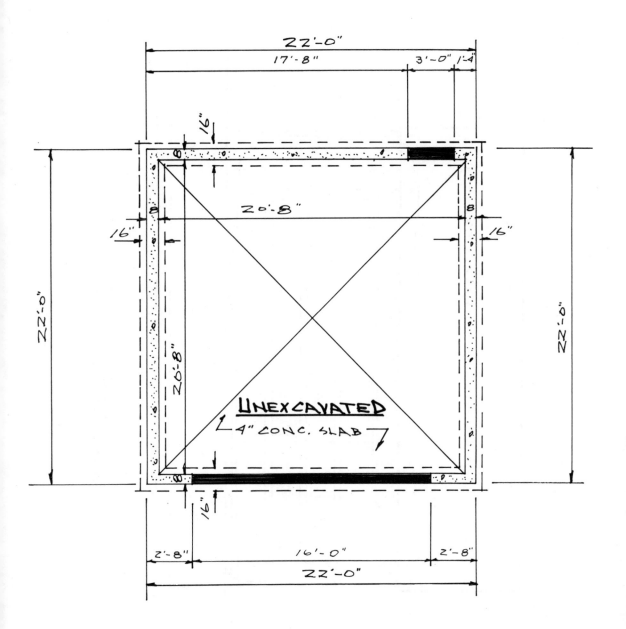

FOUNDATION PLAN

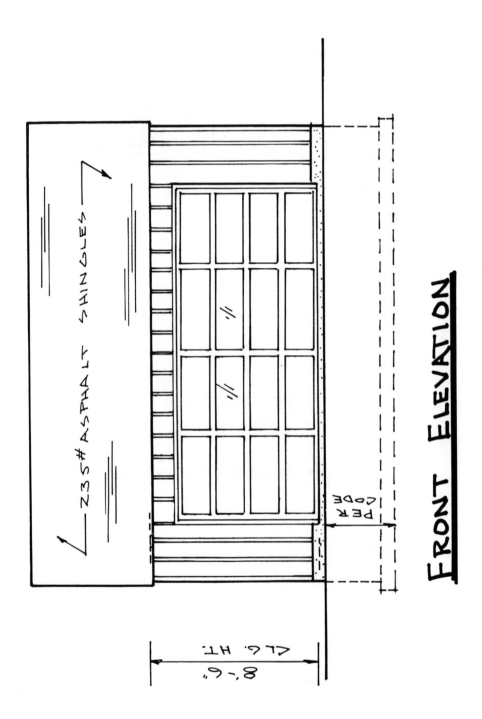

235# ASPHALT SHINGLES

FRONT ELEVATION

PER CODE

CLG. HT.

8'-6"

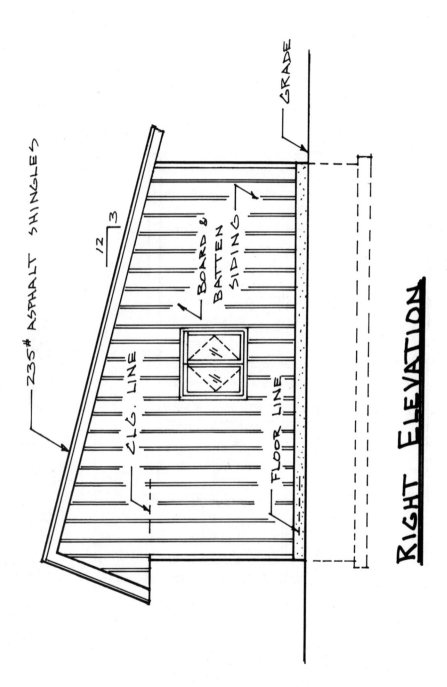

235# ASPHALT SHINGLES

12 3

BOARD & BATTEN SIDING

GRADE

CLG. LINE

FLOOR LINE

RIGHT ELEVATION

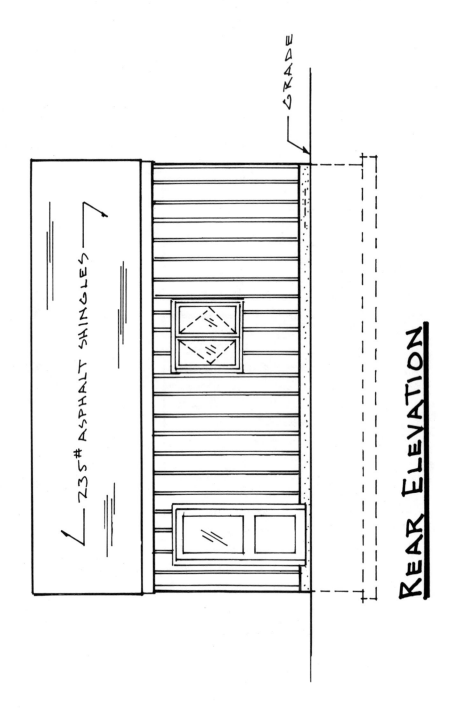

235# ASPHALT SHINGLES

GRADE

REAR ELEVATION

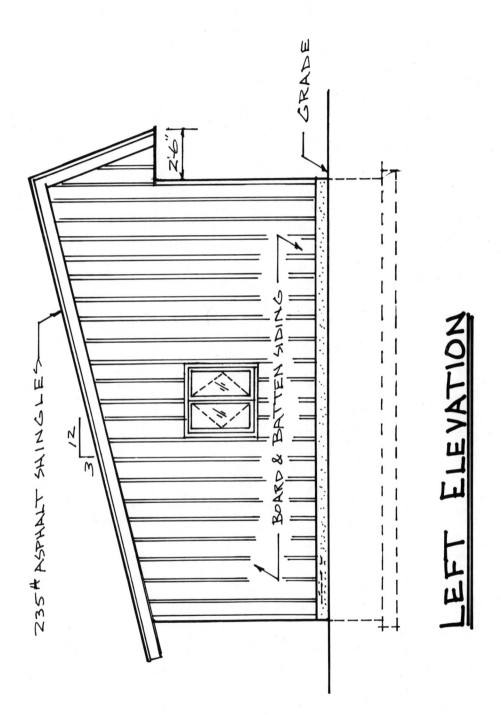

GRADE

2'6"

235# ASPHALT SHINGLES

12
3

BOARD & BATTEN SIDING

LEFT ELEVATION

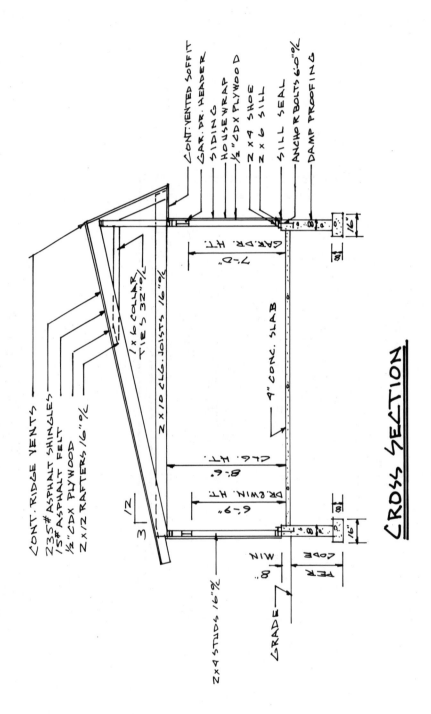

CROSS SECTION

CONT. RIDGE VENTS
235# ASPHALT SHINGLES
15# ASPHALT FELT
½" CDX PLYWOOD
2 x 12 RAFTERS 16" o/c

CONT. VENTED SOFFIT
GAR. DR. HEADER
SIDING
HOUSEWRAP
½" CDX PLYWOOD
2 x 4 SHOE
2 x 6 SILL
SILL SEAL
ANCHOR BOLTS 6'-0" o/c
DAMP PROOFING

1 x 6 COLLAR TIES 32" o/c
2 x 10 CLG. JOISTS 16" o/c

GAR. DR. HT.
7'-0"

4" CONC. SLAB

CLG. HT.
8'-6"

DR. & WIN. HT.
6'-9"

2 x 4 STUDS 16" o/c

GRADE

8" MIN

PER CODE

16"

8"

8"

16"

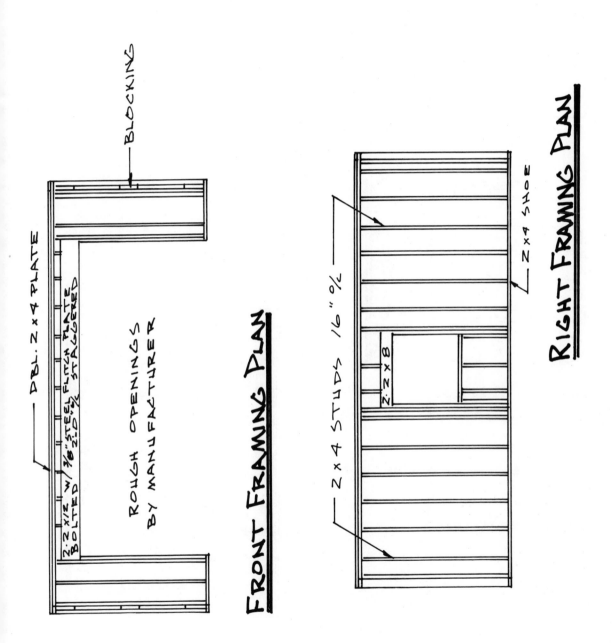

BLOCKING

DBL. 2 x 4 PLATE

2.2 x 12 W/ ⅜" STEEL FLITCH PLATE
BOLTED 2'-0"% STAGGERED

ROUGH OPENINGS
BY MANUFACTURER

FRONT FRAMING PLAN

2 x 4 SHOE

2 x 4 STUDS 16" %

2. 2 x 8

RIGHT FRAMING PLAN

121

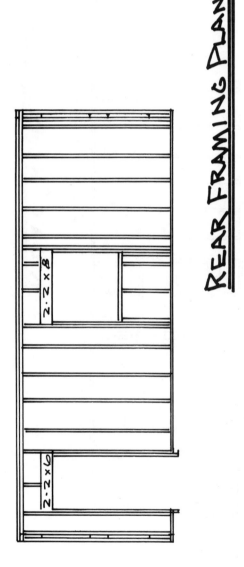

REAR FRAMING PLAN

2-2x8

2-2x6

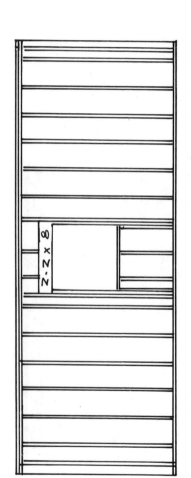

LEFT FRAMING PLAN

2-2x8

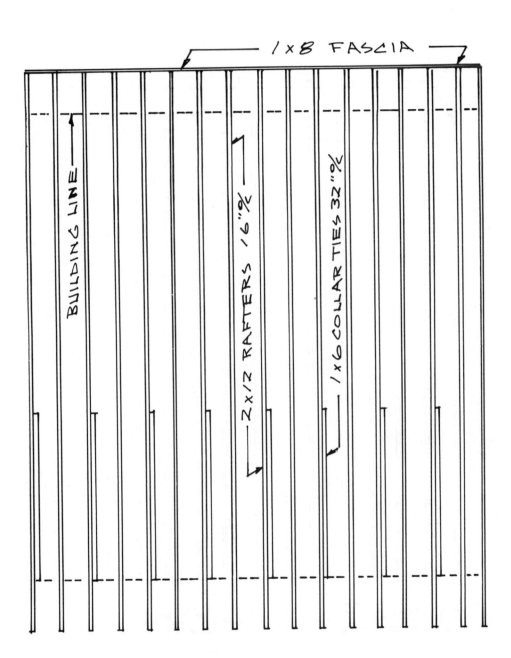

ROOF FRAMING PLAN

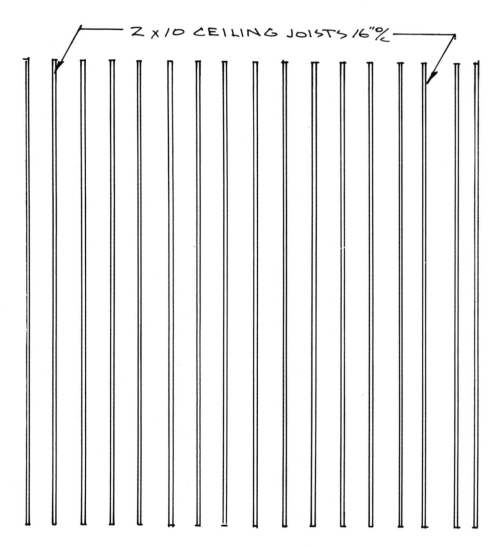

2 x 10 CEILING JOISTS 16"%

CEILING FRAMING PLAN

MATERIAL LIST
The Shawn

2 × 6 Sill----------72 lineal feet
Sill Seal-----------72 lineal feet
Anchor Bolts--------14
2 × 4 Shoe----------72 lineal feet
Double 2 × 4 Plate-----144
    lineal feet
2 × 4 Studs--------75/8--18/5
Door Headers
      2 × 12---2/18
      2 × 6---1/6

Window Headers
      2 × 8-----3/8
½″ × 4′ × 8′ Sheathing----
  21 sheets

Housewrap-------651 square feet
Siding-------------651 square feet
2 × 10 Ceiling Joists----17/22
2 × 12 Rafters--17/22
1 × 16 Collar Ties----8/8
¼″ × 24″ soffit-----6/8
1 × 8 Fascia--------3/8
1 × 8 Rake Fascia----6/10
Shingles-----------22 bundles
Asphalt Felt--------2 rolls
½″ × 4′ × 8′ Roof Sheathing
  -----22 sheets
Drip Edge------------5/10

NELSON

The Nelson is a three-car garage with three, equally-spaced overhead garage doors. It has a walkout door in the rear and three windows, which provide natural light. By using 2-inch × 8-inch ceiling joists with web support, lally columns and a beam are omitted. The hip roof has a $^5/_{12}$ pitch.

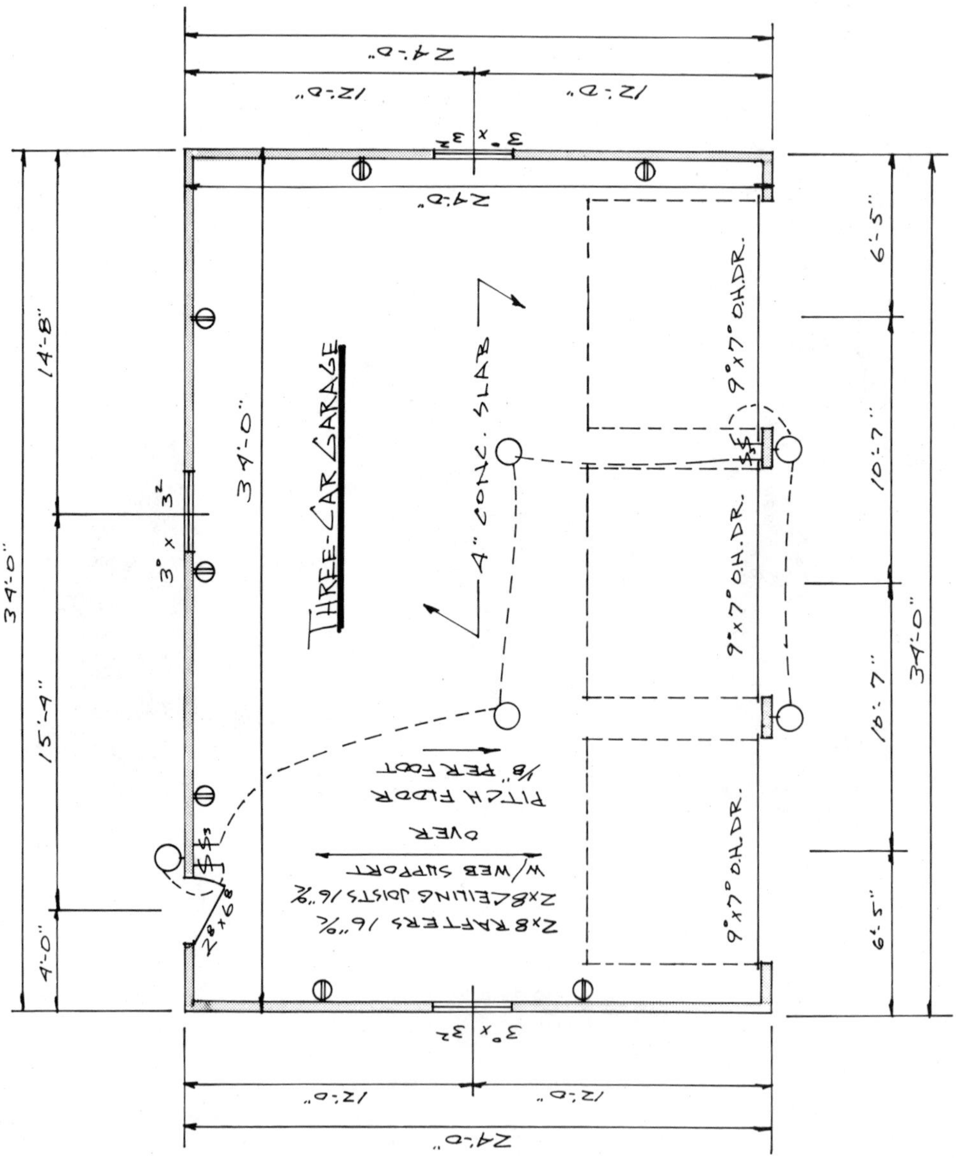

FLOOR PLAN

THREE-CAR GARAGE

4" CONC. SLAB

2x8 RAFTERS 16" o/c
2x8 CEILING JOISTS 16" o/c
w/ WEB SUPPORT
OVER
PITCH FLOOR
1/8" PER FOOT

9'x7" O.H. DR.

9'x7" O.H.DR.

9'x7" O.H.DR.

3" x 3"

3" x 3"

24'-0"

12'-0"

12'-0"

24'-0"

6'-5"

10'-7"

10'-7"

6'-5"

34'-0"

4'-0"

15'-9"

14'-8"

34'-0"

2x6x8

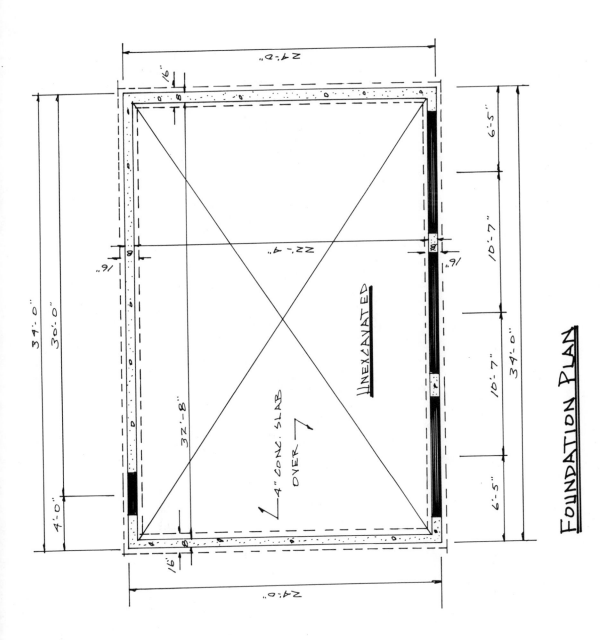

FOUNDATION PLAN

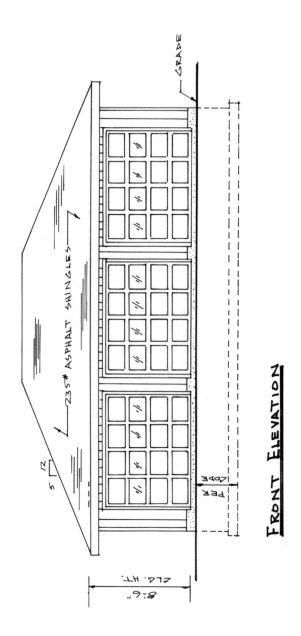

FRONT ELEVATION

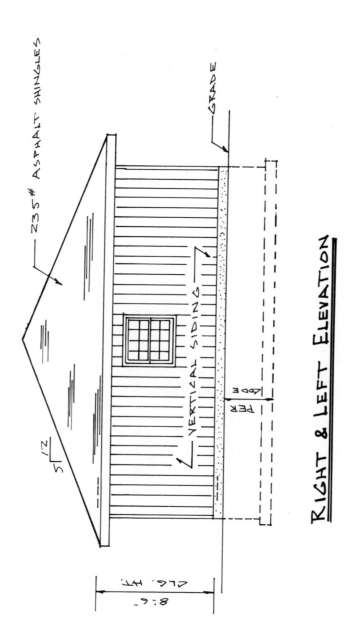

235# ASPHALT SHINGLES

VERTICAL SIDING

GRADE

PER CODE

5 | 12

8:6"

9'6" HT.

RIGHT & LEFT ELEVATION

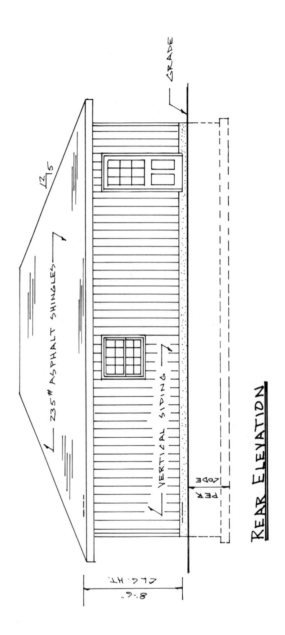

REAR ELEVATION

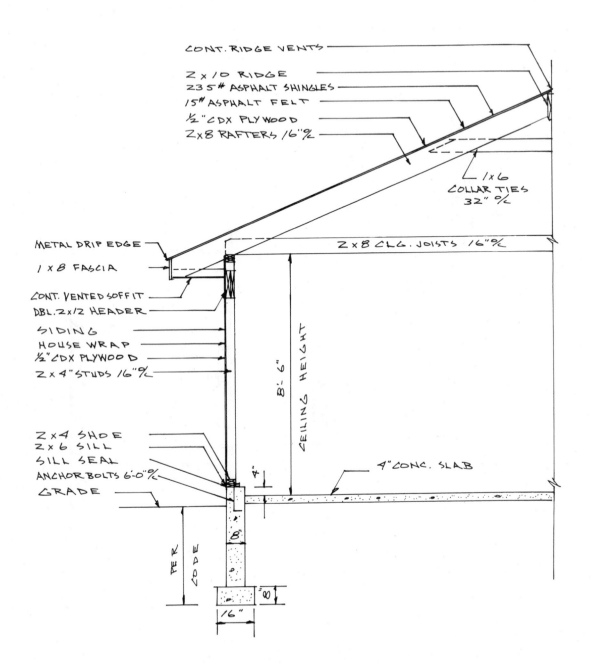

CONT. RIDGE VENTS

2 x 10 RIDGE
235# ASPHALT SHINGLES
15# ASPHALT FELT
½" CDX PLYWOOD
2 x 8 RAFTERS 16" ℀

1 x 6
COLLAR TIES
32" ℀

METAL DRIP EDGE

1 x 8 FASCIA

2 x 8 CLG. JOISTS 16" ℀

CONT. VENTED SOFFIT
DBL. 2 x 12 HEADER

SIDING
HOUSE WRAP
½" CDX PLYWOOD
2 x 4" STUDS 16" ℀

8'-6"
CEILING HEIGHT

2 x 4 SHOE
2 x 6 SILL
SILL SEAL
ANCHOR BOLTS 6'-0" ℀
GRADE

4"

4" CONC. SLAB

PER CODE

8"

8"

16"

STAFF SECTION

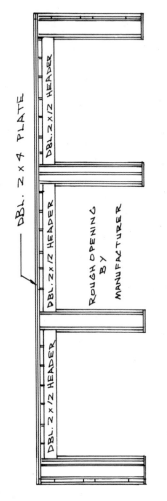

DBL. 2 x 4 PLATE

DBL. 2 x 12 HEADER

DBL. 2 x 12 HEADER

DBL. 2 x 12 HEADER

DBL. 2 x 12 HEADER

ROUGH OPENING
BY
MANUFACTURER

FRONT FRAMING PLAN

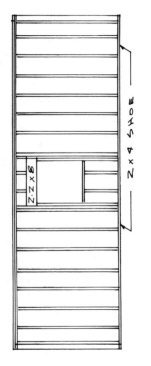

2 x 4 SHOE

2 x 2 x 8

RIGHT FRAMING PLAN

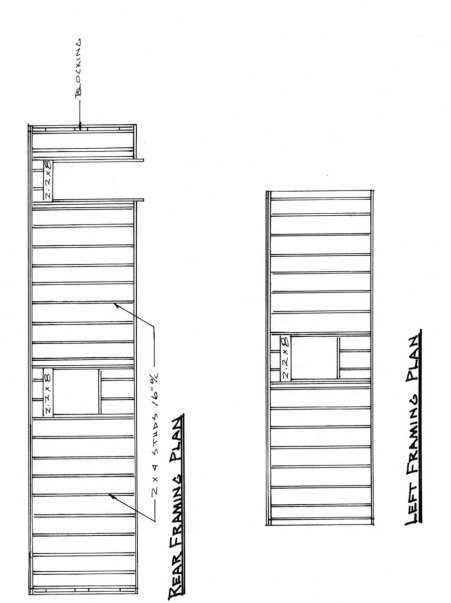

BLOCKING

2.2 x 8

2 x 4 STUDS 16" %

REAR FRAMING PLAN

2.2 x 8

LEFT FRAMING PLAN

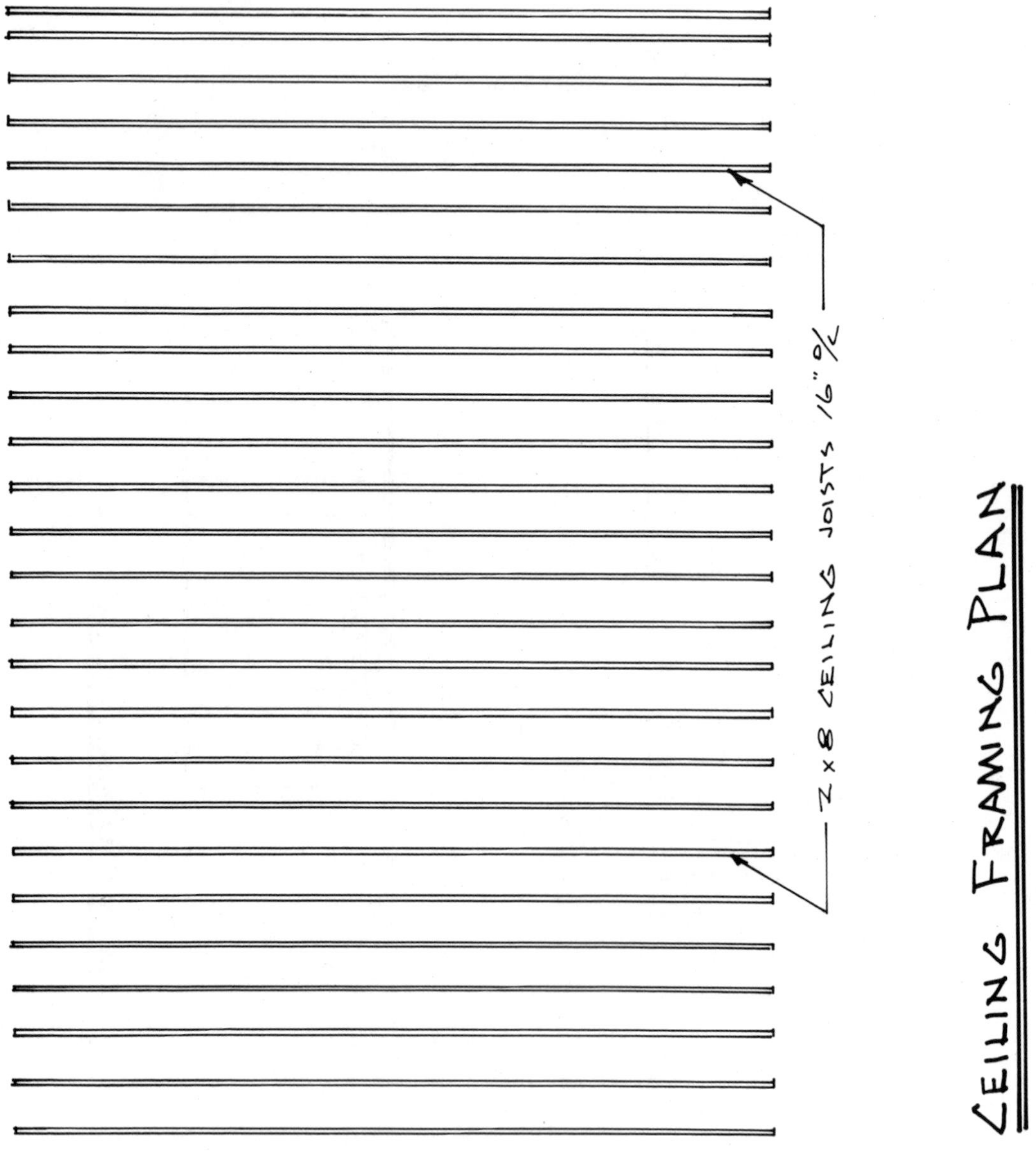

2 x 8 CEILING JOISTS 16" O/C

CEILING FRAMING PLAN

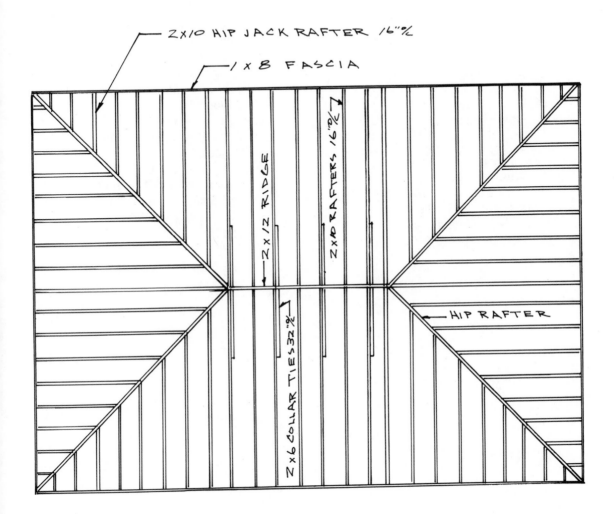

ROOF FRAMING PLAN

MATERIAL LIST
The Nelson

2 × 6 Sill---------6/12---1/14
Sill Seal---------86 Lineal Feet
Anchor Bolts-------18
2 × 4 Shoe---------6/12---1/14
Dbl. 2 × 4 Plate---9/10---1/8
2 × 4 Studs--------92/8
Door Headers
    2 × 12----6/10
    2 × 8----1/6

Window Headers
    2 × 8-----1/14---1/8
½" × 4' × 8' Sheathing
  ----20 Sheets
Housewrap-------640 square feet

Siding-------------640 square feet
Ceiling Joists----26/24
2 × 8 Rafters------16/16
1 × 6 Collar Ties--4/8
Shingles-----------33 bundles
2 × 12 Ridge 1/10
Asphalt Felt-------3 rolls
½" × 4' × 8' sheathing (roof)
  ---34 sheets
Drip Edge----------12/10
1 × 8 Fascia--------10/12---1/12
¼" × 24" Soffit----16/8---1/4
2 × 8 Hip Rafters----4/20
2 × 8 Hip Hack Rafters----16/12

CONNOLLY

The Connolly is a 26 × 26 two-car garage with living quarters above. The beam and lally columns are positioned so that they do not interfere with car placement.

The living area is designed with electric heat in mind. If you prefer another type of heat, a chimney will have to be added to accommodate the furnace flue. The water heater and the furnace can be located beneath the stairs.

The kitchen in the upper-level living quarters has a door leading to a deck, which is also accessible by a set of stairs. The bedroom has adequate closet space and cross ventilation, which is provided by two, double-hung windows. The dining/living area has a storage closet and a picture window that offers a view of the driveway area. Other features include a washer and dryer, full bath with linen closet, guest closet, and a storage closet.

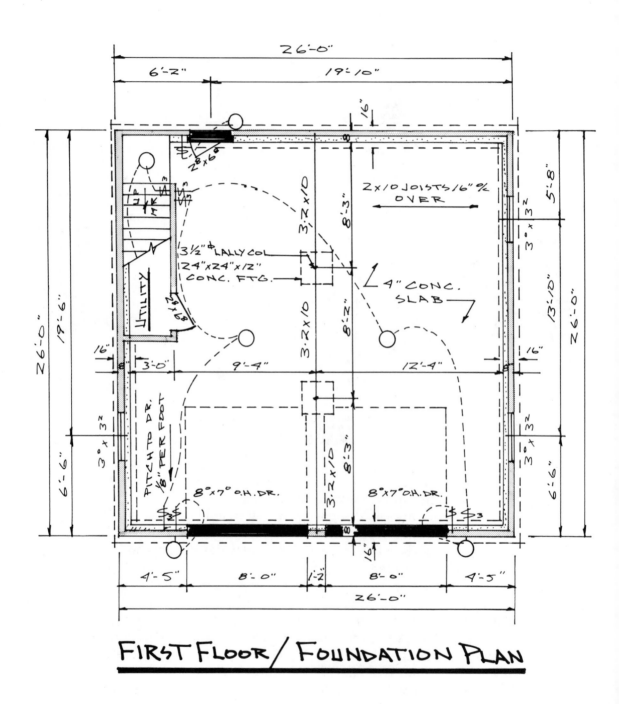

FIRST FLOOR / FOUNDATION PLAN

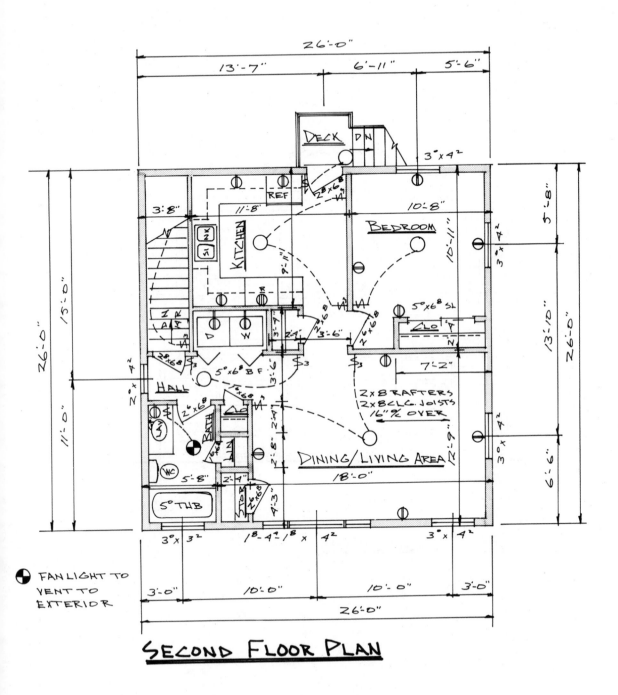

SECOND FLOOR PLAN

⊕ FAN LIGHT TO
VENT TO
EXTERIOR

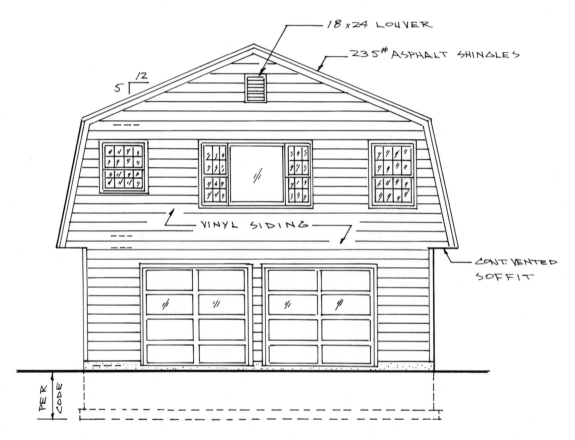

18 x 24 LOUVER

235# ASPHALT SHINGLES

5 |‾12

VINYL SIDING

CONT. VENTED SOFFIT

PER CODE

FRONT ELEVATION

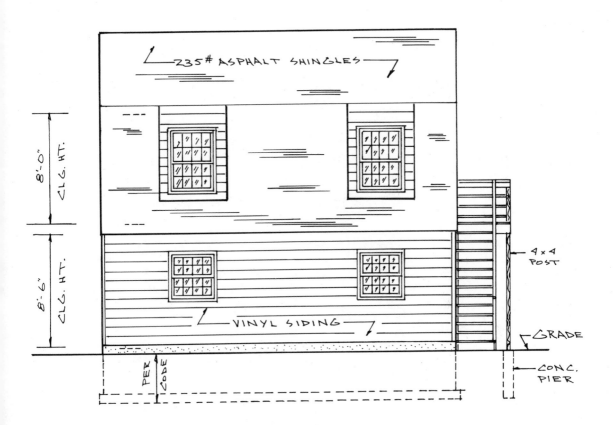

235# ASPHALT SHINGLES

8'-0" CLG. HT.

8'-6" CLG. HT.

VINYL SIDING

4 x 4 POST

GRADE

CONC. PIER

PER CODE

RIGHT ELEVATION

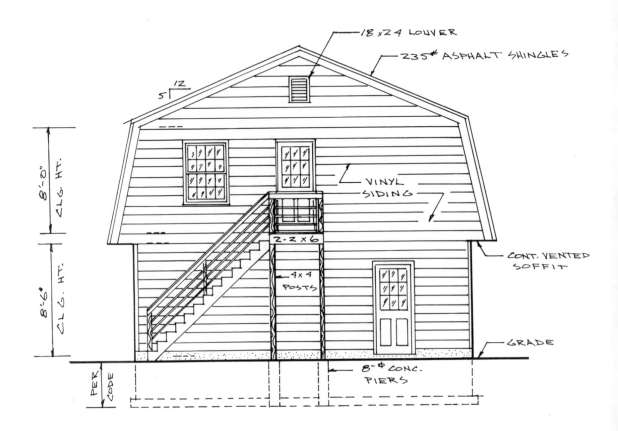

18 x 24 LOUVER

235# ASPHALT SHINGLES

12
5

VINYL SIDING

CONT. VENTED SOFFIT

2·2×6

4×4 POSTS

GRADE

8'-0" CLG. HT.

8'-6" CLG. HT.

PER CODE

8"⌀ CONC. PIERS

REAR ELEVATION

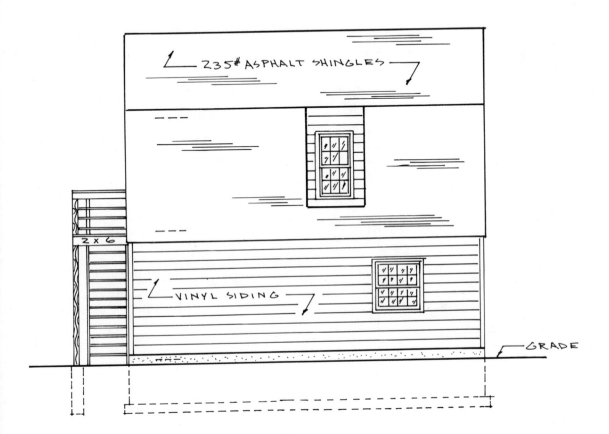

235# ASPHALT SHINGLES

2 x 6

VINYL SIDING

GRADE

LEFT ELEVATION

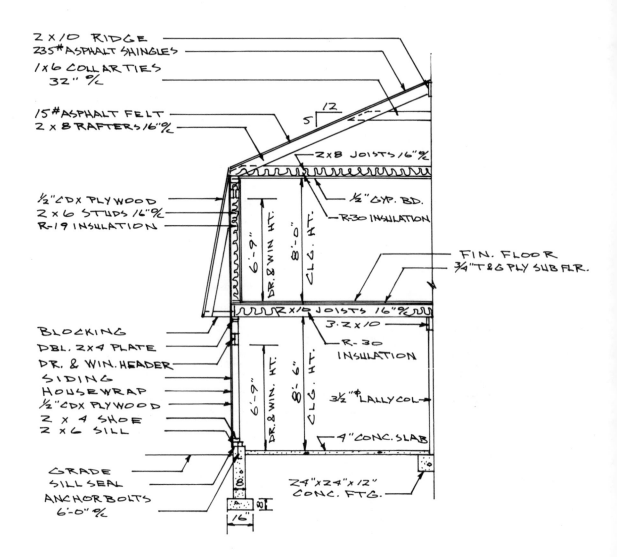

2 X 10 RIDGE
235# ASPHALT SHINGLES
1 X 6 COLLAR TIES
    32" %

15# ASPHALT FELT
2 X 8 RAFTERS 16" %

5 / 12

2 X 8 JOISTS 16" %

½" CDX PLYWOOD
2 X 6 STUDS 16" %
R-19 INSULATION

½" GYP. BD.

R-30 INSULATION

FIN. FLOOR
¾" T & G PLY SUB FLR.

6'-9" DR. & WIN. HT.

8'-0" CLG. HT.

BLOCKING
DBL. 2 X 4 PLATE
DR. & WIN. HEADER
SIDING
HOUSEWRAP
½" CDX PLYWOOD
2 X 4 SHOE
2 X 6 SILL

2 X 10 JOISTS 16" %
3 - 2 X 10
R-30 INSULATION

3½" ∅ LALLY COL.

6'-9" DR. & WIN. HT.

8'-6" CLG. HT.

4" CONC. SLAB

GRADE
SILL SEAL
ANCHOR BOLTS
    6'-0" %

8"

16"

24" X 24" X 12"
CONC. FTG.

STAFF SECTION

146

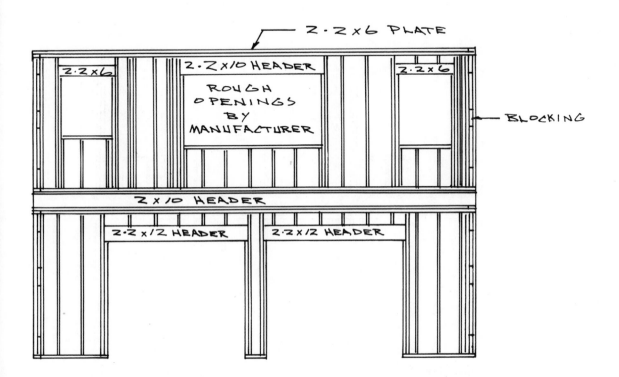

2 · 2 x 6 PLATE

2 · 2 x 6

2 · 2 x 10 HEADER
ROUGH
OPENINGS
BY
MANUFACTURER

2 · 2 x 6

BLOCKING

2 x 10 HEADER

2 · 2 x 12 HEADER   2 · 2 x 12 HEADER

FRONT FRAMING PLAN

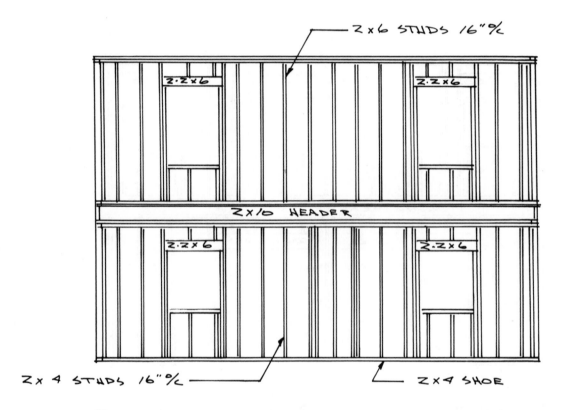

2 x 6 STUDS 16" ⁰/c

2·2x6

2·2x6

2 x 10 HEADER

2·2x6

2·2x6

2 x 4 STUDS 16" ⁰/c

2 x 4 SHOE

RIGHT FRAMING PLAN

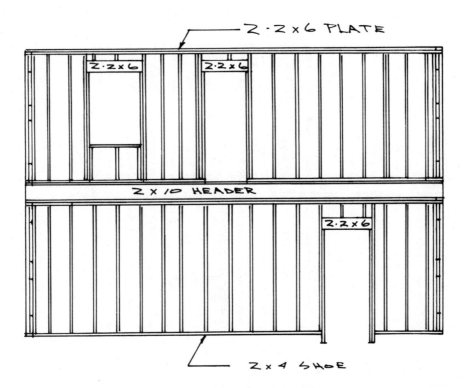

2·2 x 6 PLATE

2·2 x 6

2·2 x 6

2 x 10 HEADER

2·2 x 6

2 x 4 SHOE

REAR FRAMING PLAN

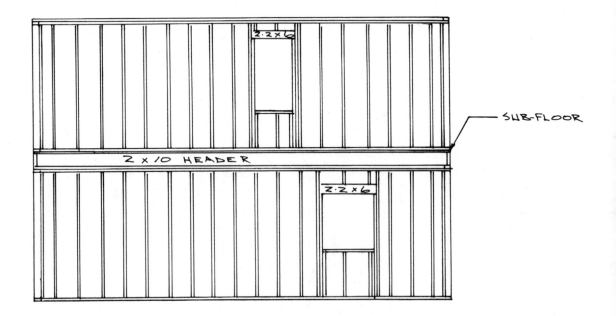

2·2×6

2 x 10 HEADER

SUB-FLOOR

2·2×6

LEFT FRAMING PLAN

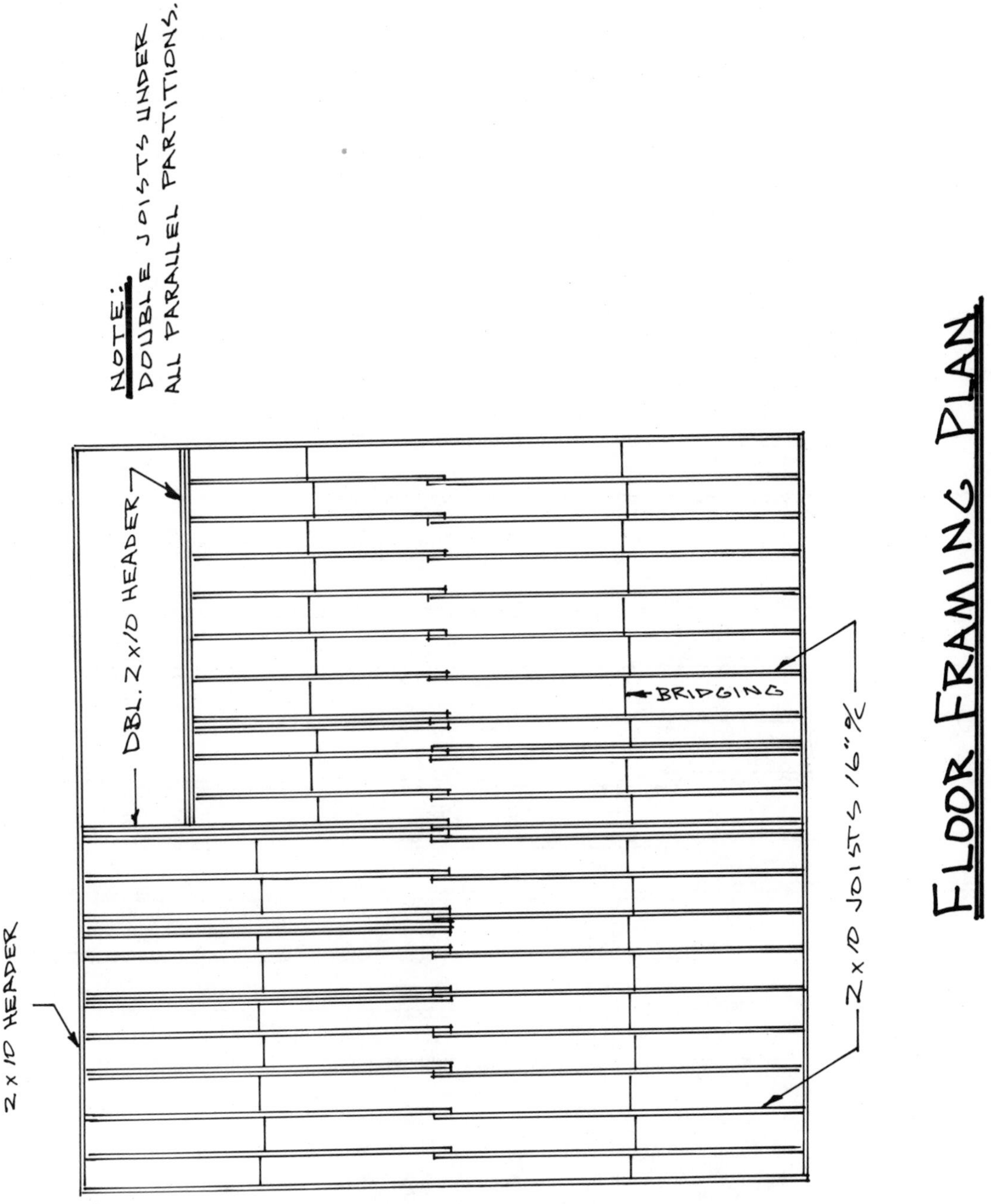

NOTE:
DOUBLE JOISTS UNDER
ALL PARALLEL PARTITIONS.

DBL. 2x10 HEADER

BRIDGING

2x10 JOISTS 16" OC.

2x10 HEADER

FLOOR FRAMING PLAN

2x8 CEILING JOISTS 16" o/c

CEILING FRAMING PLAN

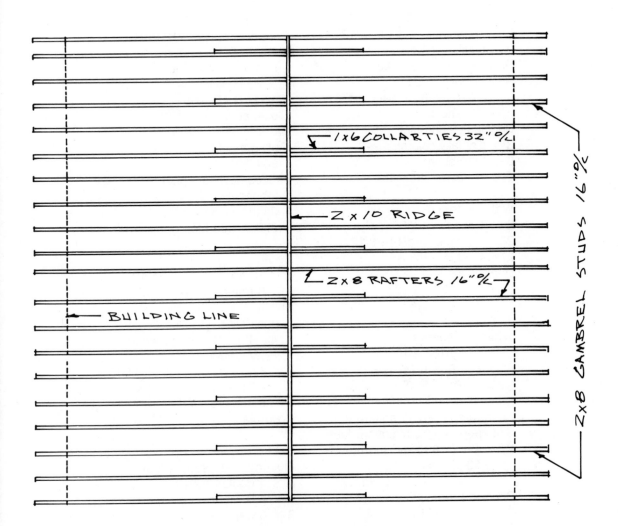

1x6 COLLAR TIES 32" O/C

2 x 10 RIDGE

2 x 8 RAFTERS 16" O/C

BUILDING LINE

2x8 GAMBREL STUDS 16" O/C

ROOF FRAMING PLAN

MATERIAL LIST
The Connolly

Floor System
2 × 10 joists----40/14---10/10
2 × 10 header-----2/14---2/12
2 × 6 sill-----8/12
Sill seal-----95 lineal feet
Anchor bolts-----21
½″ × 4'-0″ × 8'-0″ plywood
-----20 sheets
Bridging-----38 pairs
3½″ dia. lally columns-----2
3-2 × 10 beam-----
2/14---2/16---1/6---1/8

Wall System
2 × 4 shoe-----8/12
2-2 × 4 plate-----8/14---8/12
2 × 4 studs-----88/8
Door headers
2 × 12-----4/10
2 × 6-----1/6

Window headers
2 × 10-----2/10
2 × 6-----6/14---1/6
½″ × 4'-0″ × 8'-0″ plywood
-----52 sheets
Housewrap-----1641 square feet
Siding------------1307 square feet
½″ × 4'-0″ × 8'-0″ gypsum board
-----52 sheets

Second Floor
2 × 6 shoe-----1-/10---1/4
2-2 × 6 plate-----20/10---1/8
2 × 6 studs-----105/8
Ceiling joists-----
9/20---11/16---11/12---9/10
R-19 insulation
Walls-----15 rolls
Floor-----14 rolls

Interior
2 × 4 studs-----75/8
Door headers-----3/12---3/10
½″ × 4'-0″ × 8'-0″ gypsum
board-----73 sheets
1 × 12 shelving-----
1/12---1/10---1/8
Closet pole-----1/10
Baseboard-----248 lineal feet
Ceiling moulding-----
304 lineal feet
Firecode gypsum board-----
22 sheets
R-30 insulation-----
676 square feet

Roof
2 × 10 ridge-----1/14---1/12
2 × 8 rafters-----40/14
Shingles-----35 bundles
Asphalt felt-----3 rolls
½″ × 4'-0″ × 8'-0″ plywood
-----36 sheets
1 × 8 rake fascia-----4/14---4/10
¼″ × 24″ soffit-----6/8---1/4
2 × 8 gambrel studs-----40/10
Collar ties-----10/8

Decks
Flooring-----16 square feet
4 × 4 Posts-----2/10
2 × 4 Railings-----3/12
2 × 6 Cap-----3/4

Deck Stairs
2 × 12 Stringer-----2/14
2 × 10 Treads-----3/12---1/4
1 × 8 Risers-----3/12---1/8
2 × 4 Stair rail-----4/12
2 × 6 Stair cap-----1/12

BRACCIO

The Braccio is a three-car garage with living quarters above. The 26-foot width provides adequate room for a second story floor plan, while providing added storage/work area in the garage.

The length has been increased to provide room for stairs leading to the apartment above. A utility room could be located under the stairway.

A beam is necessary to support the floor joists. The lally columns supporting the beam are strategically placed to allow easy access of cars. Because of the spacing of the lally columns, it is necessary to have a beam consisting of four 2×10.

The second floor consist of two bedrooms, each with adequate closet space. The spacious living room has generous window area overlooking the garage entrance. The dinette, which is adjacent to the kitchen, has an exterior exit to a deck which is accessible by stairs. A full bath, a washer and dryer, and a guest closet complete the floor plan.

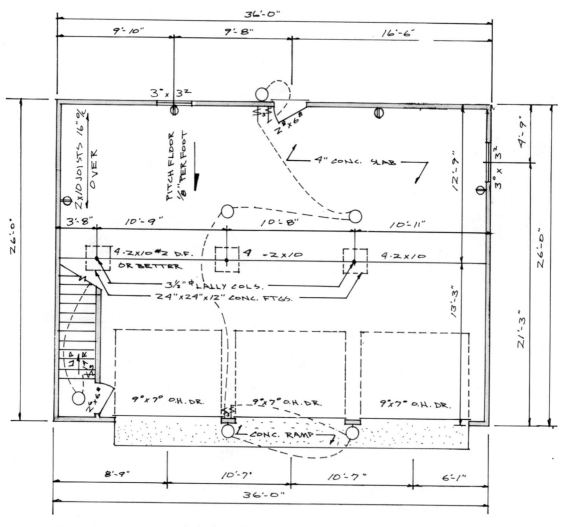

FIRST FLOOR PLAN

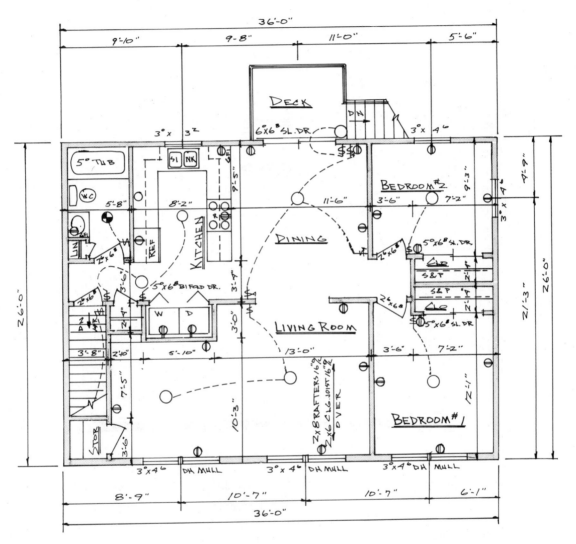

Second Floor Plan

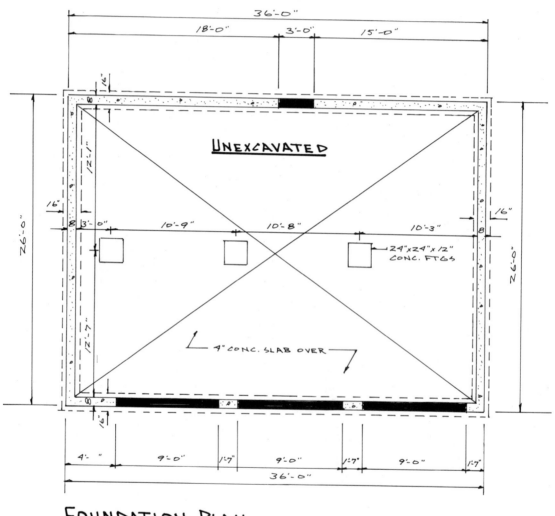

FOUNDATION PLAN

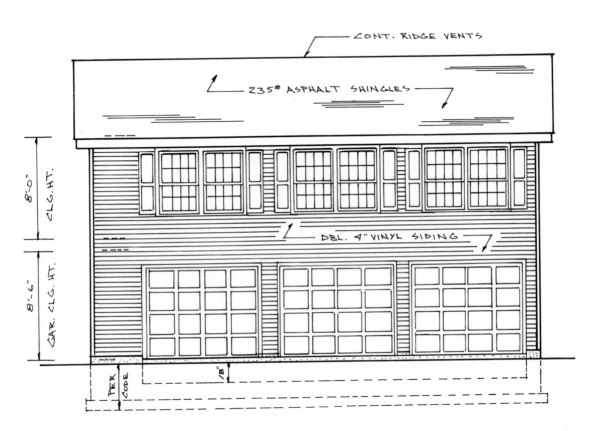

CONT. RIDGE VENTS

235# ASPHALT SHINGLES

DBL. 4" VINYL SIDING

8'-0" CLG. HT.

8'-6" GAR. CLG. HT.

PER CODE

18"

FRONT ELEVATION

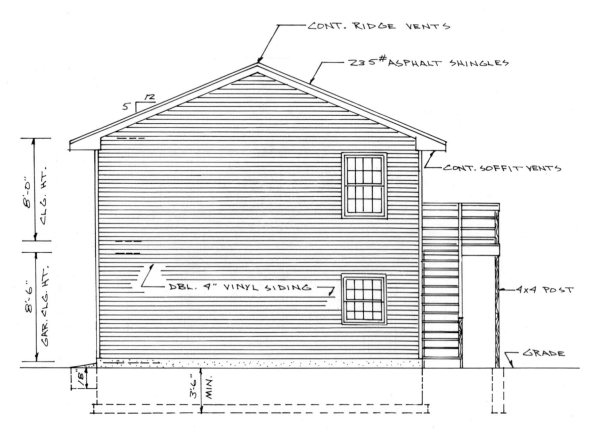

CONT. RIDGE VENTS

235# ASPHALT SHINGLES

CONT. SOFFIT VENTS

5 | 12

8'-0" CLG. HT.

8'-6" GAR. CLG. HT.

DBL. 4" VINYL SIDING

4x4 POST

GRADE

1/8"

3'-6" MIN.

RIGHT ELEVATION

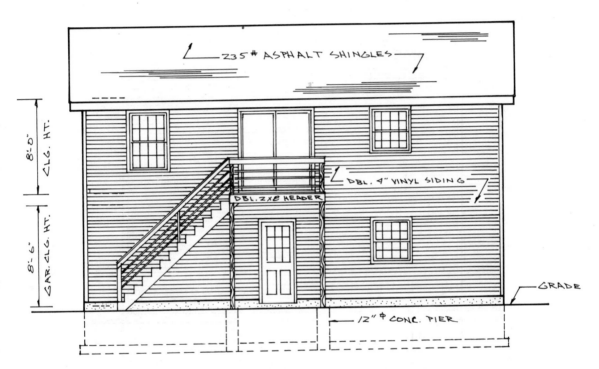

235# ASPHALT SHINGLES

8'-0" CLG. HT.

8'-6" GAR. CLG. HT.

DBL. 4" VINYL SIDING

DBL. 2×8 HEADER

GRADE

12"∅ CONC. PIER

REAR ELEVATION

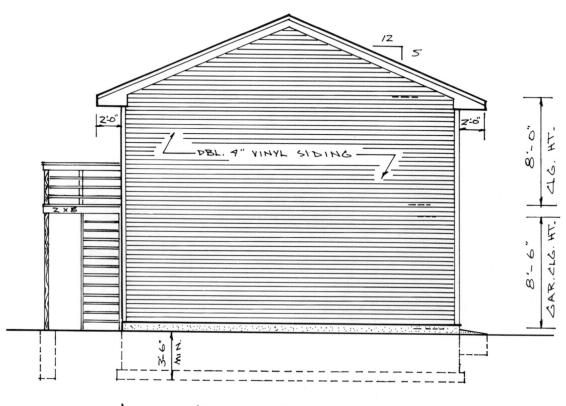

DBL. 4" VINYL SIDING

2 X 8

2'-0"

2'-0"

12
5

8'-0"
CLG. HT.

8'-6"
GAR. CLG. HT.

3'-6"
MIN.

LEFT ELEVATION

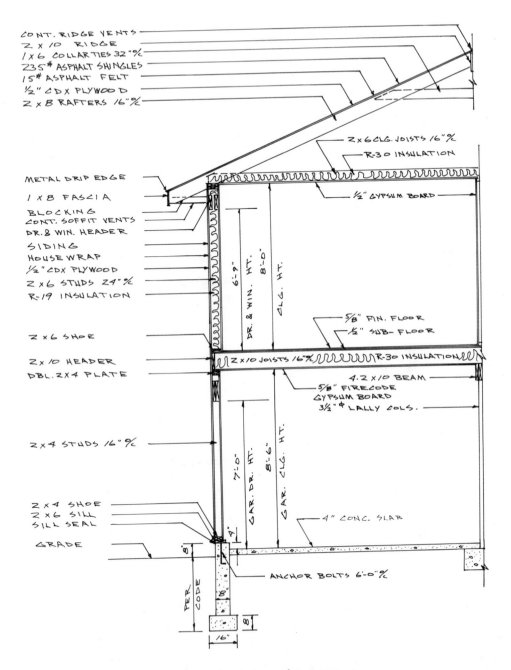

CONT. RIDGE VENTS
2 X 10 RIDGE
1 X 6 COLLAR TIES 32" O/C
235# ASPHALT SHINGLES
15# ASPHALT FELT
½" CDX PLYWOOD
2 X 8 RAFTERS 16" O/C

2 X 6 CLG. JOISTS 16" O/C
R-30 INSULATION

½" GYPSUM BOARD

METAL DRIP EDGE

1 X 8 FASCIA
BLOCKING
CONT. SOFFIT VENTS
DR. & WIN. HEADER
SIDING
HOUSE WRAP
½" CDX PLYWOOD
2 X 6 STUDS 24" O/C
R-19 INSULATION

6'-9" DR. & WIN. HT.
8'-0" CLG. HT.

⅝" FIN. FLOOR
½" SUB-FLOOR

2 X 6 SHOE

2 X 10 HEADER
DBL. 2 X 4 PLATE

2 X 10 JOISTS 16" O/C   R-30 INSULATION

4. 2 X 10 BEAM
⅝" FIRECODE GYPSUM BOARD
3½"ø LALLY COLS.

2 X 4 STUDS 16" O/C

7'-0" GAR. DR. HT.
8'-6" GAR. CLG. HT.

4" CONC. SLAB

2 X 4 SHOE
2 X 6 SILL
SILL SEAL

GRADE

4"
8"

ANCHOR BOLTS 6'-0" O/C

PER CODE
8"
8"
16"

STAFF SECTION

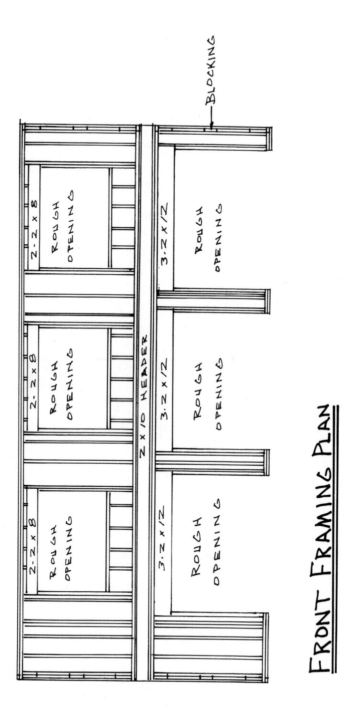

BLOCKING

2 - 2 x 8
ROUGH OPENING

2 - 2 x 8
ROUGH OPENING

2 - 2 x 8
ROUGH OPENING

2 x 10 HEADER

3 . 2 x 12
ROUGH OPENING

3 . 2 x 12
ROUGH OPENING

3 . 2 x 12
ROUGH OPENING

FRONT FRAMING PLAN

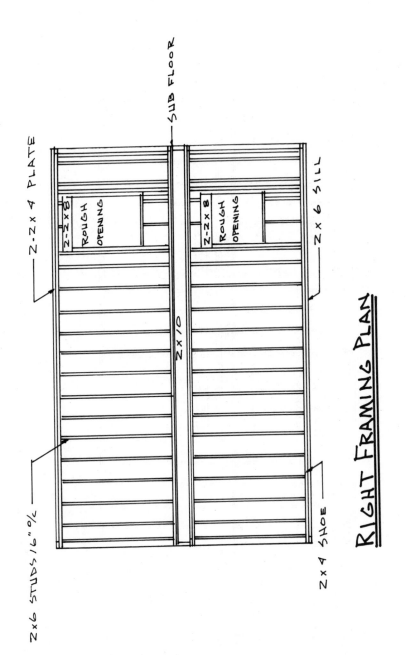

RIGHT FRAMING PLAN

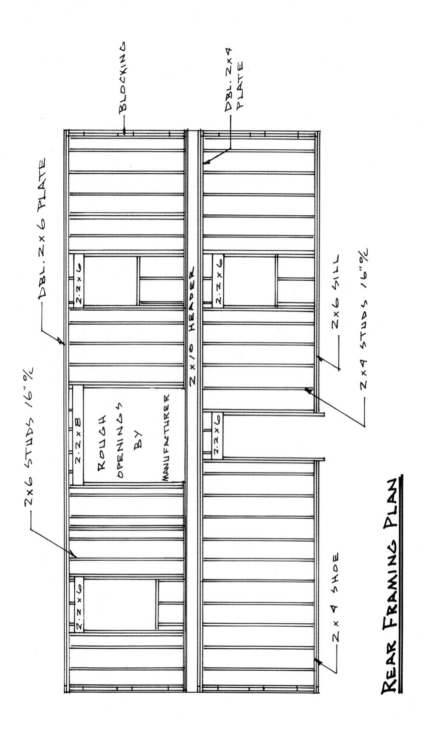

REAR FRAMING PLAN

2 x 6 SHOE

SUB FLOOR

2 X 10 HEADER

LEFT ELEVATION

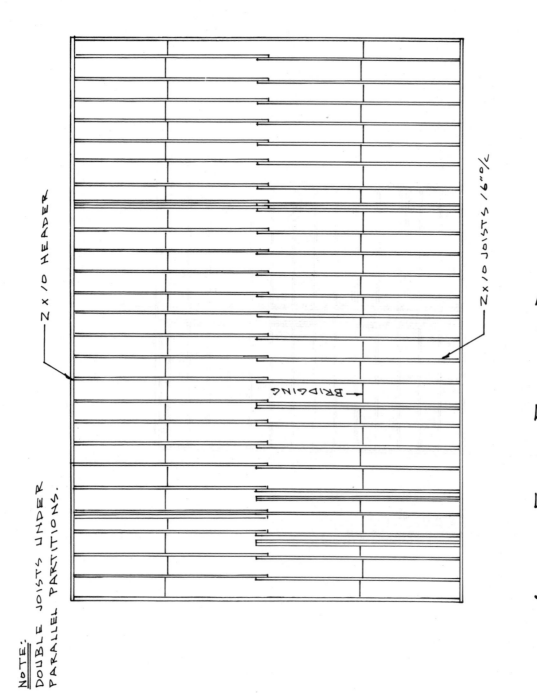

2 X 10 HEADER

2 X 10 JOISTS 16" O/C

BRIDGING

NOTE:
DOUBLE JOISTS UNDER
PARALLEL PARTITIONS.

SECOND FLOOR FRAMING PLAN

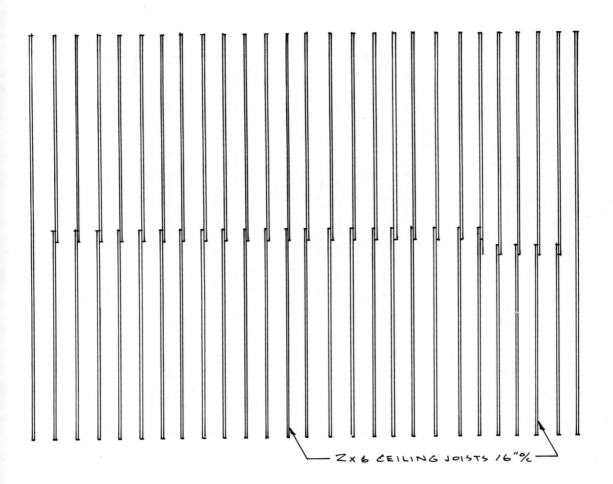

— 2x6 CEILING JOISTS 16"%

CEILING FRAMING PLAN

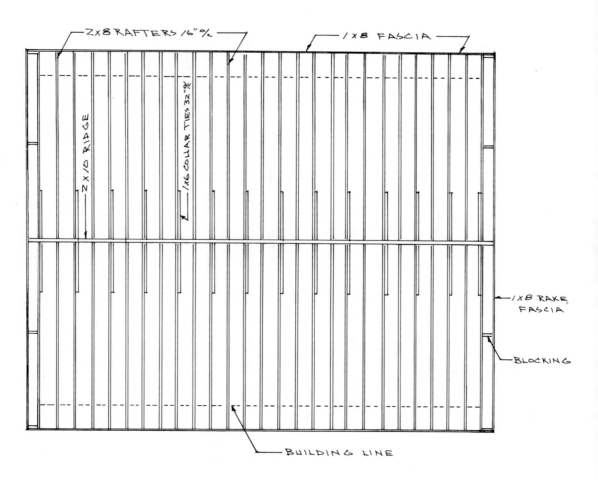

ROOF FRAMING PLAN

MATERIAL LIST
The Braccio

Lower Level
2 × 6 Sill----------7/12---1/10
Sill Seal-----------94 lineal feet
Anchor Bolts--------21
2 × 4 Shoe----------
  2/14---5/12----1/10
Double 2 × 4 Plate----
  4/14---16/12
2 × 4 Studs---------96/8
3½″ Diameter Lally Cols.----3
4-2 × 10 Beam 10/12----4/6

Second Floor
2 × 10 Joists-------62/14
2 × 10 Header--------6/12
Bridging-------------52 pairs
2 × 6 Shoe---------8/12---2/14
Double 2 × 6 Plate-----
  16/12---4/14
2 × 6 Studs---------115/8
Door Headers
    2 × 12----9/10
    2 × 8----1/14
    2 × 6----1/6

Window Headers
    2 × 8----3/14
    2 × 6----2/14---1/8
½″ × 4′ × 8′ Sheathing----
  55 sheets
Housewrap----------
  1739 square feet
R-19 Insulation---17 rolls
Siding------------1739 square feet
½″ × 4′ × 8′ Firecode
  Gypsum Board----30 sheets
R-19 Floor Insulation----19 rolls
R-30 Insulation----936 square
  feet

Interior
·2 × 4 Studs--------136/8

Door Headers
    2 × 6---3/12
    2 × 4---2/10
½″ × 4′ × 8′ Gypsum Board----
  78 sheets
1″ × 12″ Shelving----1/14---1/10
Closet Pole----1/16
Baseboard---------299 lineal feet
Ceiling Moulding----374 lineal feet
2 × 12 Stair Stringers-----2/14
Stair Risers--------3/12---1/6
Stair Treads-----3/12---1/4

Deck Stairs
2 × 12 Stringers----2/14
Risers------------3/12---1/6
Treads------------3/12---1/4
Railing----------3/14
Cap-------------1/14

Deck
Flooring----------48 square feet
4 × 4 Posts-------2/10
2 × 4 Railing-------4/8---8/6
2 × 6 Cap----------1/8---2/6
Double 2 × 8 Header----2/8
2 × 8 Joists-------7/6

Roof
2 × 10 Ridge-------2/12---1/14
2 × 8 Rafters------54/18
1 × 6 Collar Ties----14/8
Shingles------------38 bundles
Asphalt Felt--------3 rolls
½″ × 4′ × 8′ Sheathing-----
  38 sheets
Drip Edge----------8/10
1 × 8 Fascia-------1/14---2/12
¼″ × 24″ Soffit-----1/14---2/12
1 × 8 Rake Fascia-----4/16
¼″ × 12″ Rake Soffit------4/16

Glossary

Aggregate—A mixture of different mineral substances separable by mechanical means.

Bullfloat—Used to remove excess water from the surface of concrete.

Conduit—Thin-walled steel pipe in which cable is enclosed.

Countersink—To enlarge the upper part of a hole to receive the head of a screw, bolt, etc.

Framing Square—Serves as a reference when laying out rafters and computing board feet. Available in polished nickel, copper and blued finishes.

Frost Level—Depth of freezing of the soil.

Jack Stud—A shorter stud on each side of the door or window which supports the header.

Ledger—Board on which joists are fastened.

Plumb Bob—A heavy pointed weight which is suspended from a length of string to determine true plumb.

Polyethylene—Vapor barrier which separates the slab from the ground and limits vapor transmission while also serving as a water stop.

Screed—A two by four wood member which is used to pull excess concrete off the forms. The board should be straight and longer than the width of the forms.

T-Brace—Consist of two-foot length of one by four wood member nailed to two by four upright. Total length is to be $1/2$ inch longer than the floor to ceiling height.

Index

Index